Can Journalism Be Saved?

Rediscovering America's Appetite for News

Rachel Davis Mersey

 PRAEGER

AN IMPRINT OF ABC-CLIO, LLC
Santa Barbara, California • Denver, Colorado • Oxford, England

Library of Congress Cataloging-in-Publication Data

Mersey, Rachel Davis, 1978–
    Can journalism be saved? : rediscovering America's appetite for news / Rachel Davis Mersey.
        p. cm.
    Includes bibliographical references and index.
    ISBN 978-0-313-39208-5 (hard copy : alk. paper) — ISBN 978-0-313-39209-2 (ebook)   1. Journalism—United States—History—21st century.
2. Journalists—United States—History—21st century.   I. Title.
    PN4867.2.M47   2010
    071'.309051—dc22   2010011356

ISBN: 978-0-313-39208-5
EISBN: 978-0-313-39209-2

14   13   12   11   10   1   2   3   4   5

This book is also available on the World Wide Web as an eBook.
Visit www.abc-clio.com for details.

Praeger
An Imprint of ABC-CLIO, LLC

ABC-CLIO, LLC
130 Cremona Drive, P.O. Box 1911
Santa Barbara, California 93116-1911

This book is printed on acid-free paper ∞

Manufactured in the United States of America

To my husband, Jason, and my parents, Deirdre and Jack

Contents

Illustrations

Preface

I began in 2004, after a few years of working as a journalist at the *Arizona Republic* in Phoenix, research on bringing young adults back to newspapers. I was immediately confronted with the words of a professor who became one of my mentors. Philip Meyer, author of the *Vanishing Newspaper* and *Precision Journalism,* challenged me to focus on a problem that could actually be solved. He was not, I realized after a year into the doctoral program at the University of North Carolina at Chapel Hill, pushing me to another research area altogether but encouraging me to shed my industry-based preconceptions and to think of what I was interested in via a relevant framework.

With Meyer's encouragement and the support of so many others—Rhonda Gibson, my dissertation co-chair; Dan Sullivan, a visiting professor at Chapel Hill during my time there; and faculty inside and outside my discipline—I found that framework: social identity. I have spent the years since fleshing out its relevance in the media industry. My dissertation, which was completed in 2007, revealed a disconnect between social responsibility of the press theory and online journalism.

This book attempts to fill that gap with a new model. "The search for a future for serious reporting is the journalism story of our time," wrote *Columbia Journalism Review* Executive Editor Mike Hoyt in the September/October 2009 issue. This book is about that future. To this point, figuring out how to preserve journalism's community-service function under the social responsibility model has consumed the industry's attention. The preponderance of this attention has focused on how to fund the vital work of the Fourth Estate, monetizing content on the Web being the key issue. In summer 2009 the Newspaper Association of America solicited several technologies companies, including Google, to develop strategies for success with paid content on the Web. However, even the most innovative—and perhaps profitable—of these approaches proposed by these companies and others throughout the industry are focused on answering the wrong question. The wrong question: "How can journalism companies pay for the community-based work they have always done?" The right question: "How can the work of journalists evolve to serve Americans today?" This book is about answering that question.

Acknowledgments

In academia there is the sense that you are cut from the cloth worn by your mentors. If this is true, there is no more beautiful cloak than that composed of those who have shepherded my work. Thank you to Philip Meyer of the University of North Carolina at Chapel Hill. Phil introduced me to academic research of journalism and has kept me excited about it from the beginning. Thank you to Rhonda Gibson, also of UNC-Chapel Hill, who taught me to believe fiercely in the importance of theory and the clarity of writing. Thank you to Dan Sullivan of the University of Minnesota. He challenged my ideas with thoughtfulness and innovative perspectives. Thank you to Frank Mulhern of Northwestern University who brought the most important question of this book to the forefront: "Should journalism be saved?" And thank you to David Abrahamson, also of Northwestern University, who convinced me that there was a book to be done here and walked me through every step of the writing and publishing process.

Working at an institution like Northwestern University affords so many opportunities but also means there have been a great number of contributors to this work. I first thank the Medill School of Journalism administration, Dean John Lavine and Associate Dean Mary Nesbitt, for their support of my scholarly pursuits. They gave me the intellectual space to challenge the old way of doing things, and I continue to appreciate that very much. I've also been able to bounce ideas off some of the brightest people in education today, people who provided support, pushed my thinking, and in some cases became co-authors on other work. Thank you to those colleagues: Clarke Caywood, Jack Doppelt, Rich Gordon, Craig LaMay, Donna Leff, Ed Malthouse, Abe Peck, and Charles Whitaker. In addition, to all the graduate and undergraduate students who have asked bright questions and engaged with these concepts, thank you, especially to Allison Stevens (MSJ, 2010) who read every word of this book and provided comment and encouragement.

Finally, thank you to all the journalists, especially my friends at the *Arizona Republic,* who continue to work tirelessly on behalf of their communities. I believe their work is very important, and I believe this book provides a path to helping that work have the impact it merits.

PART ONE

Journalism and Democracy Are Dead

CHAPTER 1

A Brave New World of Journalism

All our knowledge has its origins in our perceptions.
—Leonardo da Vinci

This book asks, "Can journalism be saved?" It is an apt question in a news environment marred by budget cuts, layoffs, and newsroom closures. At this point in the national conversation about the future of news, which extends from dozens of academic and professional conferences to a 2009 Senate hearing convened by U.S. Senator John Kerry, the one thing that need not be revisited is the failure of newspapers. Only more names should be added to the list of the demised: Denver, Colorado's *Rocky Mountain News* in February 2009, New Mexico's *Albuquerque Tribune* in the same month, and Arizona's *Tucson Citizen* in March 2009. Their obituaries are speckled with a variety of causes of death: Cities can no longer support two newspapers; there is no market for afternoon papers in an Internet environment; no buyer can be found. With this deep level of trouble plaguing the news business, a precursor question must really be posed: "Should journalism be saved?" While journalists scoff at even considering the alternative—imagining a dark, bleary, corrupt, watchdog-less world—asking "should journalism be saved" and "if yes, why" must be the first steps if its purported value is to be preserved.

Journalists and journalism advocates often cite the history and status of the profession as justification for its necessity in public life and to democracy, and their conversations have expanded exponentially as new interpretations of *public life* and new theories of democracy have been brought to bear. What remains true is that the roots of journalism are a part of this "should journalism be saved" discussion and specific attention should be given to the relevant history of the models of journalism being practiced. For the first two hundred years of its history, news was the propriety of Colonial printers and then political parties. Chain ownership emerged in full force at the beginning of the 20th century. At that time, technological changes, such as the Linotype machine and the rotary press, and business forces, in particular national advertising, took hold and the nation had its first press barons. By the 1930s the six largest newspaper chains—Gannett, Hearst, Patterson-McCormick, Paul Block, Ridder, and Scripps-Howard—controlled more than two-thirds of the nation's daily circulation. This era was also favorable for the growth of other news media. *Time* magazine entered the market in 1923. Within 10 years, competitors *Newsweek* and *U.S. News & World Report* launched. The reach of the barons, a list that now included *Time* co-founder Henry Luce, only continued to stretch via radio, a nonprint channel and thereby not constrained by the geographic coverage of the transportation system in the country at that time.

The important point is that news, as it was practiced beginning in the early 1900s, was professionally created and commercially distributed. Examples abound. Edward R. Murrow joined CBS in 1935 and ascended to the anchor seat of the network's evening news in the 1950s, a seat he notably used to rebuke U.S. Senator Joseph McCarthy in a personal manner that marked a departure from television's facts-first approach to the news during this time. Influential columnist Walter Lippmann, co-founder of the *New Republic* and author of the lauded book *Public Opinion*, used his professional position, in part, to argue that public affairs were too complex for the average citizen, and that society needed to be governed by an intelligence class. Years later, in the 1970s, Bob Woodward and Carl Bernstein exemplified investigative reporting of this era with their series on Watergate, which led to President Richard Nixon's resignation and the *Washington Post* being awarded the Pulitzer Prize for Public Service, journalism's highest honor.

Because of the depth and breadth of their work, journalists during the first three-quarters of the 20th century can be conceptualized as part of the influence model, which was conceived by Hal Jurgensmeyer, a Knight Ridder executive, in the 1970s. The influence model prized the societal influence of newspapers as a journalistic output that is not for sale, as opposed to the output that is for sale such as the newspaper itself or its advertising space. Think of it in this way: There are many inputs into a newspaper including personnel; newsprint; electricity for the buildings, computers, and operations; the computers themselves and associated technological services; and other overhead. There are two outputs: societal influence, which is not for sale, and commercial influence, which is for sale. Societal influence comprises the ability of a newspaper to get its readers to trust it. Commercial influence, on the other hand, attends to the newspaper's capacity to circulate effectively via subscriptions and single-copy sales, and motivate people's decisions to make other purchases—groceries, clothing, and cars, for example—thereby attracting advertisers of such goods. Of course, societal influence and commercial influence are intertwined because it is the former that gives the latter any value. A newspaper with absolutely zero societal influence will not be able to sell copies nor attract advertisers.

An important extension of the influence model was that it provided business justification for quality journalism. Philip Meyer of the University of North Carolina at Chapel Hill, who introduced me to the influence model in 2004, explained: "If the model works, an influential newspaper will have readers who trust it, and therefore it will be worth more to advertisers."[1] There was based on this line of reasoning incentive to invest in the news product. Proportionately large reporting budgets and staff sizes were indicative of the third quarter of the 20th century. Beyond the anecdotal—what Woodward and Bernstein's Watergate coverage did for the *Washington Post*—there was evidence that the influence model worked. Although not the most determinative factor of circulation, superior newspaper quality as measured by judges' ranking correlated with increased circulation for newspapers.[2] We also know that trust in the press was at its height during this time based on evidence from the National Opinion Research Center's General Social Survey, but the data indicate that the press ultimately did not fare well across time. It is therefore important to examine potential internal and external sources of this downslide.

Journalists in the top-down influence model took direct responsibility for the quality of their news products. It is important to point out that these journalists likely had no conscious understanding of their roles in the higher-order influence model; however, through the limited channels of mass communication available, they were gatekeepers. News selection and production relied on the execution of professional processes of reporting and editing institutionalized in journalism. Newscaster David Brinkley's oft-quoted comment from an April 11, 1964, *TV Guide* interview, news is "what I say it is," summed up journalists' approach to their work—and their pervasive sense of elitism—during this time. Despite journalists' level of influence on the news agenda and the public, in 1970 the concept of the influence model was rocked. U.S. daily newspaper circulation fell below the total number of American households for the first time in history, a trend from which the industry has never recovered.

Arguments about what trigged this downward shift in circulation ran the gamut: overall disinterest in news caused by political disengagement and the multiplication of media choices; perceived reduction in leisure time due to population shifts from the city centers to the suburbs and associated increase in commuting time; the increase in both the number of single-parent households and the percentage of women in the workplace. What is clear is that newspaper readership, a once-institutionalized behavior of the American adult, was being discarded. More than three-quarters of adults, 77.6 percent, read a newspaper on an average weekday in 1970, according to aggregate data from the Newspaper Association of America. The number was less than 70 percent in 1980 and continued to trend downward to less than 65 percent in 1985.[3]

In addition to readers' abandonment of the print newspaper during this time, technology began slowly changing the processes of creating and distributing news. By 1980 a *U.S. News & World Report* article headline asked, "TV News Growing Too Powerful?"[4] And this was still while the first 24-hour news network, Cable News Network (CNN), the brainchild of Ted Turner, was just being introduced with an initial $20 million investment. While the first years of CNN were marked by poor video quality and inexperienced reporters—departures from the professional standards of news production of the previous era—audience members valued the ability to get news on their schedule. They were no longer tied to the networks' evening timeslots and the delivery of their local daily newspaper. CNN continued to grow as a real news competitor to more established outlets when it delivered on-the-ground footage of breaking news events: the assassination attempt that wounded President Ronald Reagan in 1981; Cuba's May Day celebration the same year, which was the first television broadcast from that country for an American audience; and the blow-up of the space shuttle *Challenger* in 1986, an event that was to Generation X what the assassination of President John F. Kennedy was to baby boomers. In addition to bringing ongoing live coverage to bear, CNN's presence in the marketplace meant news outlets that were confined by the time of the 30-minute newscast or the space of the printed page were challenged by a new beast free from these constraints.

But CNN's success coincided not with the expansion of news but with the modulization of news. Tidbits of news in the form of infographics, short stories, and audio or video bites became commonplace. *USA Today*, which became the industry leader in this more colorful, more entertaining segment of the news genre, launched in 1982.

Then, of course, came the revolution that was—that is—the Internet. The Internet alone is not responsible for the changes in journalism. Clearly newspaper readership was on the decline years before high-pitch tones launched dial-up connections, and cable broadcast outlets including CNN and MSNBC, which went on air in 1996, had long challenged the nightly network news. However, the Internet is a powerful enough force on the changes in production and consumption of media to be on the short list of things that must be discussed in reference to the future of news. Because the Internet offers minimal cost to entry, as opposed to the expensive printing presses owned and operated by media companies, the magnitude of information available online trumps any and all newspapers—and their archives. But beyond the pure amount of material, one of the primary differences between the natures of the content is that the Internet opens a channel for nonprofessional producers. That means the *New York Times* online, which also was launched in 1996, is available alongside citizen-produced Web logs or blogs. Of course, only in the most rare circumstances— the *Drudge Report* and the *Huffington Post* as examples—do Web-based communications rise to the level of impact as measured by reach that institutional news Web sites do, but the very presence of this array of citizen-produced online Web sites in the marketplace clearly matters. There is now more information and channels of communication competing for users' attention, and new online outlets have the competitive advantages of speed of production and immediate access to their readers (for print) or users (for the Web).[5]

In addition to hosting the rapid proliferation of new competitors in the marketplace, the last 30 years have seen undeniable changes in the economics of the news media related to deregulation, consolidation, and the trend toward public ownership. Relaxation of the Federal Communications Commission's (FCC) ownership policy under President Reagan encouraged several high-profile media mergers. In 1985 Capital Cities Communications purchased the much larger ABC to become what was then the largest media merger in the nation's history. The new Capital Cities/ABC had extensive holdings in newspapers, magazines, and television and radio stations. About 10 years later, the Walt Disney Company broke the previous merger record when it purchased Capital Cities/ABC. During that intervening decade, General Electric acquired RCA and with it NBC, and Westinghouse Electric Company bought CBS. As a consequence, local ownership of media entities decreased. By the early 21st century there were only 12 independently, family-owned newspapers with a circulation of more than 100,000 in the entire country. Media critics including Robert McChesney and Ben Bagdikian have rightly argued that these economic changes have negatively impacted the news products, citing sameness in news selection across properties; a reduction in the number of unique editorial voices, a trend exacerbated by layoffs across the news business; an increase in the amount and depth of conflicts of interest between news outlets and their parent companies; and further reduction in the news hole—the time or space allotted for news content—with more resources being dedicated to cross-promotion of like-owned properties. Consider that Julie Chen of CBS's *Early Show*, a morning news program, has been hosting one of the network's reality shows *Big Brother* every season since it launched in 2000, each time using her *Early Show* co-anchor position to invite the houseguests, or contestants, for an interview the day after they are evicted. It is an example of not only time-absorbing cross-promotion but also a journalist being extended into a conflict of interest.

The corporatization of media has also led to an increasing focus on earnings. And because revenue for news Web site advertising has fallen well short of offsetting the rapid and deep loss in revenue for print advertising, many news companies have responded with personnel and production cost cuts. Beyond the obvious closures, there has been much evidence of these troubling financial times. The Tribune Company, owner of newspapers (including *Chicago Tribune*, the *Los Angeles Times*, the *Baltimore Sun*, the *Orlando Sentinel*, and the *Hartford* [Connecticut] *Courant*), and television and radio stations (including WGN America on national cable and Chicago's WGN-AM), declared bankruptcy in 2008.[6] The *Star Tribune* in Minneapolis, owned by the private equity firm Avista Capital Partners, filed for Chapter 11 bankruptcy protection in 2009. That was less than two years after Avista purchased the paper for $530 million from the McClatchy Company, which paid $1.2 billion for the *Star Tribune* in 1998. Also in 2009, Philadelphia Newspapers, owner of the *Philadelphia Inquirer* and the *Philadelphia Daily News*, declared bankruptcy. There have been newsroom job cuts at these troubled properties and others across the country—often more than a 50-percent reduction in newsroom staffs, such was the case at the *Baltimore Sun*, the *San Francisco Chronicle*, and the *Los Angeles Times*. As another means towards cost cutting, more than one hundred daily newspapers have eliminated print production at least one day a week. As yet another alternative, the *Detroit News* and *Detroit Free Press* reduced home delivery to three days a week. All these changes have significantly reduced the news coverage in these communities. And, for now, online coverage of local news via personal blogs and even more professionalized Web sites has fallen short of having the level of reach and influence that these newspapers commanded even at their weakest points, an aspect that will be addressed with greater detail in chapter 5.

There have been some positive effects of this new era, which has been called participatory, on media content. Journalists are no longer in a relationship with their audience built on one-way communications as Murrow,

Lippmann, and Woodward and Bernstein were. The connection from the audience back to the journalists has now been solidified as part of the communication process. In the late 1990s the first step toward encouraging two-way communication was taken when newspapers began adding reporters' e-mail addresses to their bylines. Although not universally well received—newsrooms were then filled with journalists who never responded to readers' messages—this was a sign of things to come. Today discourse among journalists and their audience is commonplace: journalists from the Associated Press (AP), reporters and editors, respond to readers' e-mail questions about news gathering, current events, or specific studies via the "Ask AP" column; CNN's Jack Cafferty uses his platform on the *Situation Room* with Wolf Blitzer to ask questions of his viewers, choosing to read some responses on the air and posting the remainder online; and stories on the *New York Times* Web site are accompanied by any number of tools meant to engage readers including links to reporters' blogs and active online discussions, and opportunities for readers to share content via LinkedIn, Digg, Facebook, and e-mail. Beyond sharing content, people can also use the Web to draw attention to issues and perspectives they believe have inadequate or misleading coverage. For example, when a gentleman posted to YouTube a dashboard camera video of a Utah highway patrol officer using a Taser gun on him during a stop for speeding, the story was immediately picked up by ABC News and the authorities were prompted to expedite an internal investigation of the incident. The audience is in a place it has never been before—in control.

Collectively, these industry-audience changes shifted the media's approach to producing and distributing the news from Jurgensmeyer's influence model to the market model of journalism. Simply, the market model of journalism is based on tenet of demand. Give audiences what they want. The market model gets a bad rap among most journalists—the word "market" certainly is not helping its cause, but one of the primary objections is that this model reduces news to a simple commodity, no different than bread or automobiles (and post the 2009 American auto industry bailout, no one craves that comparison). Most journalists believe their work merits special privileges. Their position is supported by that fact that journalism is the only business addressed in the U.S. Constitution, a position that truly differentiates it from other privately held and publically traded companies.[7]

Let us set side aside this important point for a moment to make another, more positive observation related to the market model of journalism. In reality, some journalists know and respond to their audiences quite well. In general, they are magazine writers and editors. Magazine journalists are not afraid to craft their product for their audiences. It is in their blood because it is in their business model, creating through their magazines immersive experiences for their audiences so that they can sell space to advertisers whose advertisements then become part of the experiences. This audience orientation practiced by magazine writers and editors shares an important similarity with Jurgensmeyer's influence model: a foundation in trust. Trust in Jurgensmeyer's conception was built by providing quality, well-reported news. Trust in the case of audience-sensitive magazines is more relationship-based. Magazines aim to understand their readers well enough to provide them not only relevant and interesting content but also a thoughtfully crafted reading experience built around advertising, design, and productions values.

In fact, magazine experiences are so carefully crafted as to allow product differentiation in an incredibly crowded marketplace. Consider the abundance of epicurean magazines at your local newsstand, a crowd that remains thick even after Condé Nast announced the closure of *Gourmet*, the nation's oldest food magazine at 68 years old, in 2009. Some, but not all, of these: *Bon Appetit, Food & Wine, Everyday Food, Cooking Light, Food Network Magazine, Saveur, La Cucina Italiana, Vegetarian Times, Cook's Illustrated, Taste of Home, Cook's Country, Cooking with Paula Deen, Eating Well,* and *Everyday with Rachael Ray*. This list does not even include the season-specific and specialty magazines produced by these titles—*Taste of Home*, for example, has *Taste of Home Holiday, Simple & Delicious, Healthy Cooking,* and *Country Woman*—or the lifestyle magazines with a taste of cooking content such as *Martha Stewart Living, Family Circle, Southern Living,* and *Sunset*. Even with potentially "too many cooks in the kitchen," epicurean remains a category with high product differentiation for readers and advertisers. Each successful magazines owns its niche in the market and although the segmentation is not limitless, opportunities for differentiation still exist. *Food Network Magazine*, launched by Hearst in 2009, found a new niche of the market: food entertainment. Relying on the success of its cable channel, the magazine capitalized on the celebrities it helped create: Bobby Flay; Ina Garten, aka the Barefoot Contessa; and Guy Fieri. Even in the down market of 2009, *Food Network Magazine* hit its initial rate base—the number of readers it promised to advertisers—in an unheard-of 21 days and delivered by the end of its launch year more than 1.1 million paid subscribers.

At the other end of the category, one might say, is the venerable *Cook's Illustrated*. It has a celebrity of its own sort, Christopher Kimball, whose presence in the magazine is marked by a simple black-and-white sketch of him wearing his signature bow tie. Kimball, host of PBS's *America's Test Kitchen*, founded *Cook's Illustrated* (and its sister publication, *Cook's Coun-*

try) on a 100-percent subscriber-financed model, which now includes a paid Web site. Writing on the shuttering of *Gourmet* in a *New York Times* op-ed, Kimball defined his magazines' market niche:

> To survive, those of us who believe that inexperience rarely leads to wisdom need to swim against the tide, better define our brands, prove our worth, ask to be paid for what we do, and refuse to climb aboard this ship of fools, the one where everyone has an equal voice. Google "broccoli casserole" and make the first recipe you find. I guarantee it will be disappointing. The world needs fewer opinions and more thoughtful expertise—the kind that comes from real experience, the hard-won blood-on-the-floor kind. I like my reporters, my pilots, my pundits, my doctors, my teachers and my cooking instructors to have graduated from the school of hard knocks.[8]

Interestingly, Kimball had what he called a "head-on collision" with *Gourmet* in 1990 when Condé Nast purchased *Cook's Illustrated*, immediately ceased publication, and folded *Cook's* readership into *Gourmet's* subscription base.[9] Kimball relaunched *Cook's* in 1993 and *Gourmet* has since closed. And according to Kimball the unique selling point of his magazines in the market of readers (since his products are advertising free) is unbiased, unadulterated expertise. Kimball sounds like a traditional Murrow-Lippmann-Woodward-Bernstein journalist.

Trouble is while magazine journalists like Kimball see opportunity to sell expertise, newspaper journalists are too mired in complaints about the market model to really discuss their audiences—or dare to think about crafting products for them. Their fear is simple: People want celebrity, sports, and odd news, not national and international news; people care about themselves, not public affairs. Former *Los Angeles Times* editor John Carroll summarized: "The public, particularly the much-sought-after young reader, has an insatiable appetite for celebrity coverage. And newspaper-owning corporations are more interested these days in responding to raw market demands, no matter how demeaning, than in such old-fashioned pursuits as public service."[10] The fear is not entirely unfounded, especially among the young reader audience referenced by Carroll.

Consider the entrance of newspaper-produced tabloids to the market, which began early in this decade. The *Chicago Tribune's RedEye*, a free, commuter daily, is just one example. Shortly after its 2002 launch, *RedEye* claimed to have cracked the code for reaching adults 18 to 34 years old, a code that is clearly embedded in pictures and not in text. The good aspects of products such as these cannot be overlooked. People, mostly people who would otherwise not pick up a print news product at all, are reading. Even if the initial appeal is in the consumer news and entertainment bits, the tabloids also include local, national, and international news briefs. Eight years later, *RedEye* continues to rely on short stories, big pictures, and a news-feature mix that leans heavily toward the latter, and it has success-fully built an audience with a mean age in its early 30s. Cover stories about giveaways and discounts at Chicago bars and restaurants ("Free Love"), the proposed hike in public transportation fares ("Fare Warning"), locals marching in Washington, D.C., for gay rights ("Gay Crusade"), President Barack Obama winning the Nobel Peace Prize ("Prize or Problem?"), and Chris Rock's latest documentary ("Everybody Hates Chris?") represent a typical five-day stretch of *RedEye*'s approach. It should be noted that the *Tribune*'s competitor, the *Chicago Sun-Times*, took its turn at the "picture book" trend with *Red Streak,* which folded after a few years. *Quick* from the *Dallas Morning News* changed its format in the fall of 2008 from its initial news-features mix to focusing exclusively on entertainment and nightlife, and reducing distribution from five days a week to one. Other products that have survived along with *RedEye*—*Express* from the *Washington Post* and *Noise* from the Gannett-owned *Lansing* (Michigan) *State Journal*—have drawn harsh criticism. For example, journalist Farhad Manjoo, writ-ing for *Salon*.com, made the point: "The problem with taking solace in *RedEye*'s success is that it feels like settling for ignorance."[11] Maybe the real problem is that news companies are being ignorant to opportunities to serve their audiences with news.

Today news companies, speaking in generalization because there are a small number of exceptions, are engaged in the poor and thoughtless actualization of the market model of journalism. This is clear in the type of research the media industry is conducting. As Mike Donatello, director of research for *USA Today,* wrote: "Newspaper audience research seeks to estimate the size of individual publications' audiences, their demographic characteristics, and their product consumption and general media-use habits."[12] Audience research for television, newsmagazines, and radio is rarely richer in its insights. The result of this approach is most certainly the degradation of news products into entertainment products; it is the "sex sells" philosophy of the news business. As has been pointed out al-ready, the trend of serving the audience by giving them more of what they already read and watch has become particularly apparent as news outlets at-tempt to lure in young readers. There are many more "make them happy"—which might be more aptly called "make them buy it"—examples across platforms. In April 2008, Kathie Lee Gifford, co-host of *Live with Regis and Kathie Lee* with Regis Philbin from 1985 to 2000, joined the fourth hour of the *Today Show*. She and fellow host, Hoda Kotb, spend the final hour of the number-one watched morning *news* show gossiping, fawning over celebrities and pseudo-celebrities, and passing along beauty and diet advice. This is just one of the many examples of giving people what they want so that they watch.

The birth of prizing the reader or user in this way was actually born long before the news industry reacted to it. In 1977 Charles Fisher at Louisiana State University recognized "news is what the people want to know" as one element of his three-part definition of news.[13] In particular, Fisher pointed to the public's intrigue with "excitement and entertainment." Celebrity news, including salacious nuances, crime dramas, and political scandals all amounted to the news people wanted to hear. As a practical measure of the news people wanted to know, Fisher offered that "news is anything that people will talk about. The more it will excite comment, the greater its value." This part of Fisher's definition prized the consumer's perspective.

Since the news companies began responding with increased soft-news content with vigor at the beginning of this century, this trend has been called by some the dumbing down of the news. Journalist Charles Madigan focused on the word "journalism" to explicate these changes in the industry. Citing the insertion of humor into the news, the cross-promotion of movies, and attention to celebrities, he suggested that "journaltainment" may be more apt.[14] He also explored "journalganda"—propaganda disguised as journalism—as an alternative. Finally, Madigan offered "journography," journalism meets pornography. As examples we have South Carolina Governor Mark Sanford's south-of-the-border jaunts in 2009; New York Governor Eliot Spitzer's high-priced prostitute scandal in 2008; and, in the same year, former presidential candidate and U.S. Senator from North Carolina John Edwards's admission of an ongoing affair with one of his campaign employees and his eventual statement in January 2010 about his status as the father of her child. Collectively, Madigan's descriptors reflected a soft news, or anti-hard news, trend in the industry designed to attract young and light news consumers. Trouble is that this approach leaves too many individuals without the important news of the day required to be informed citizens.

So the real market model of journalism for serious producers of news is figuring out how to tell important stories in relevant and compelling ways with products that are sensitive to users' changing needs. For reasons that should become clear throughout this book, I call this the identity-based model of journalism. The identity-based model of journalism is not about the pandering being done by almost all the major newspapers and television stations in the country today. There is actually reason to believe that people, even those elusive 18- to 34-year-olds, are interested in what journalists might call "real news." Evidence from the Pew Research Center for the People and the Press' News Interest Index, a weekly survey designed to capture the public's interest in and reaction to major news events, indicated that "fluff" may not be universally well received. In April 2009, 53 percent of those surveyed said there had been too much coverage of President Obama's family and personal life.[15] In June 2009, fewer than 1 in 10 respondents said they followed the news related to the NBA Finals more closely than any other news story, while 13 percent said they followed the championship series very closely. The murder of a Kansas doctor who performed abortions (16 percent), President Obama's speech in Cairo (26 percent), the crash of an Air France plane off the coast of Brazil (28 percent), the bankruptcy of General Motors (29 percent), and the economy (41 percent) were all more likely to be followed very closely. In July 2009, nearly two-thirds of respondents said there was too much coverage of pop icon Michael Jackson's death. This, of course, is not to say that audiences do not have a weakness for the fast and fascinating. They most certainly do, some audiences more than others. However, their relationships with news are now more complex than ever.

To better explain this phenomenon, the Readership Institute at Northwestern University began to examine the new manner in which individuals consume news, pinpointing that people do not just read news; they experience it. In 2003 the Institute pinpointed 26 experiences that have a positive effect on newspaper readership (motivators) and 18 experiences with the opposite effect (inhibitors). Key motivators: it is a regular part of my day, it looks out for my interests, it gives me something to talk about, it makes me smarter, and it provides information about people I know. Key inhibitors: it wastes my time, I use it for skimming the headlines, it makes me feel as if I'm drowning in the news, it lacks a distinctive personality, and it has too many pages and too many stories.[16] The Medill School of Journalism, under the leadership of professors Abe Peck and Edward Malthouse, has since expanded on this idea to detail a variety of experiences individuals have with media, not just newspapers.[17] We will discuss some of these experiences and the research that led to this work in chapters 3 and 7, but the key takeaway of the idea of experience-oriented reading at this turn is that *news is not just about content*. It is also about how people use and interact with media products.

Author Eric Hodgins pinpointed the changing consumer as the crux of the need for an intelligent concept of news as early as the 1940s. Hodgins wrote: "Maybe man biting dog was news in America, once upon a time. But do you realize how old that quotation is and how long that precept has prevailed? It goes back more than three-quarters of a century into the America of the unlovely era of Reconstruction; to a world when the ordinary citizen had no means of aspiring to anything much in the way of knowledge or culture or understanding; In that world perhaps indeed the definition of news could be so trivial."[18] Cosmopolitan and informed citizens, according to Hodgins, wanted more. Even more so today, news is complicated by context, context that varies from user to user. News companies have failed to respond to these individual nuances in any material way because they are handicapped by the misinformed approach of trying to serve the whole by appealing to its lowest common denominator.

This is a consequence of the misuse of the market model of journalism that Meyer somewhat predicted in 1978.[19] In an article entitled "In Defense of the Marketing Approach"—yes, this is the same Meyer who defended the value of the influence model—he wrote, "If it could be demonstrated that the rational response to the demands of the marketplace is flashy graphics, chopped-up news summaries, and fluffy entertainment in place of solid information about public affairs, our society would indeed be in big trouble." But as Meyer went on to point out, "Such a connection has yet to be made, however. Strange and alarming things are being done to some newspapers—but the connection between the innovations and serious marketing research is either tenuous or nonexistent. The art of using scientific research in the marketing of newspapers is extremely underdeveloped and that is a pity, because the industry could use some solid cues at this moment in its history."[20] That moment has extended into an era of declining readership, and the disappointing relationship between news organizations and thoughtful research about audience needs related to news—not to demand—is still lacking. While trying to motivate buying behavior, there is no real focus from these companies on understanding what actually *motivates* news consumption, lessons media entities might use to attract readers to important local, national, and international issues. This was the failure of the news business in 1978. It remains the failure of the news business today. Newspapers, newsmagazines, and network news programming are still attempting to be *mass* media in a world where mass does not exist anymore. Fractionalization has overcome media.

Earl Wilkinson, executive director and CEO of the International Newsmedia Marketing Association (INMA), referred to this trend as "atomizing."[21] And in December 2009 he called for an audience-based perspective: "The result is a mad dash to understand the new audience segments and maximise the new value formula of 'audience+content+platform.'"[22] This book is about that "audience+content+platform" equation with the emphasis where it should be—on the audience.

But the real trouble in asking the "should journalism be saved" question posited at the beginning of this chapter is that it forces us to consider the current state of news media plagued by the news industry's failure to serve its purpose to inform the audience of important issues. Should journalism as we know it today be saved? Probably not. Journalism today is too mired by being under the control of misguided news companies. Should journalism, the best of what we have known historically that focuses on important, relevant storytelling, be saved? Absolutely yes. The trouble is that most news outlets are not situated to do the work as it needs to be done today. Their current efforts across all platforms of communication continue to be based on a completely outdated, albeit noble, sense of community-wide service. They are born of the brains of newspapermen and women; and newspapers, as we have established, are ill fated.

In one of the now many reports on the future of journalism in America, Leonard Downie of the *Washington Post* and Arizona State University, and Michael Schudson of Columbia University appropriately pointed out, "The days of a kind of news media paternalism or patronage that produced journalism in the public interest, whether or not it contributed to the bottom line, are largely gone."[23] But while Downie and Schudson, advocates of diverse sources of news to respond to changes in the newspaper marketplace, offered a number of different financial opportunities for these fledging local news organizations, they neglected to detail any new models for the news itself. The fact is that the service-based, community-first mindset is now irrelevant. That model was born out of a 19th-century conception of community; communities were distinct entities. Today communities exist across state boundaries, communities bleed into other communities, and communities exist in virtual space. There is no way to serve an entire community, or even a majority of it, with a general-circulation news product. Now individuals matter more. That is an essential shift that does not just matter to the business model, as Downie and Schudson approach the problem, but also to the creation and dissemination of news.

Me-first (or them-first, however you see it) is not a new phenomenon. Even in the journalism business we have seen the emergence of this concept. Really Simple Syndication or Rich Site Summary (RSS) feeds allow users to select and aggregate updates to news headlines and blogs in one location using free products like Google Reader. Consider that the *New York Times* offered in early 2010 about 160 RSS feeds, 31 from the op-ed section alone. Readers can select the content they are interested in having delivered and ignore the rest. Such a customization opportunity comes with just about every journalism site these days. But as this example demonstrates, the attention to individual needs in journalism has mostly been relegated to consumers' actions; they use tools to sort, select, and share. Journalists need to take charge of the audience's relationship with media in a new way.

This book presents an alternative perspective: Journalists should not care about geographic communities. These communities are "ungettable."

No product, no marketing campaign will change that. The calls for journalism to be saved because local communities need it have as a core assumption that these communities are reading, caring, and engaging. They are not. They are not because journalists have failed them. Members of these communities are engaging in new ways and their attachments, I argue, are identity driven. News organizations must understand this new reality to reinvent themselves. Former journalist Mark Briggs, now CEO of a digital-innovation company, reminds us: "There's the philosophical riddle about the tree falling in a forest when no one is around. Does it make a sound? Now try this twist: If a journalist has a story, but there is no market for news, is it worth doing?"[24] The work that is worth doing today is that which matters. Journalists' work should be driven by attracting readers to their products, whether they be print or multimedia, and ultimately getting those readers to connect with the work, its author, and one another. It is a tall task, not the write-and-disseminate model of yesteryear, which only required journalists to master the arts of news judgment and writing. The identity-based model of journalism proposed in this book requires journalists to also master the science of audience understanding. Meyer made this call in 1978 but it has yet to be realized.

The individual-first, identity-based approach proposed here rejects playing to the audience's weakness for the fast and fascinating news. The focus is about creating news products that connect individuals to topics that matter broadly in a way that matters to them personally. This book is not only about that argument but ultimately, in the final section, presents a new model of journalism based on individual needs (chapter 6). Of course this framework will not be useful in the abstract. The ever-important supporting business model (chapter 7) will be reviewed. Before that, though, the frameworks that have been in use for explaining the purpose of journalism will be examined with attention to their shortcomings based on changes in journalism, which will be the focus of chapter 2, and the changes in the audience's needs and behavior, which will be covered in chapters 3, 4, and 5.

The real purpose of being a journalist is to tell stories that inform *and* entertain. Historically, a good number of journalists have done this well. But the business of journalism—earnings, profit margins, expenses, and advertisers—has distracted news outlets from fostering their best work. News holes have been slashed. Substantive coverage has been traded in favor of senseless coverage. And efforts to innovate have been undercut by vast layoffs and financial cutbacks. News outlets have done these things on the back of the statuses afforded to them by the First Amendment and their communities, where they were once the only information powerbrokers. New competitors have changed that landscape. There are new audience needs, new conceptualizations of community, and a new sense of service. Storytelling must advance to inform *and* entertain in this new environment. Yet journalists continue to try to serve mass unconnected audiences with the old way of doing things. They have let the information sun set and the entertainment moon stay out too long. It is time for the sun to rise on a new form of journalism that begins with the audience.

CHAPTER 2

From Whence Journalists Came

Histories make men wise; poets, witty; the mathematics, subtle; natural philosophy, deep; moral, grave; logic and rhetoric, able to contend.

—Francis Bacon

The concept of social responsibility is at the heart of journalism, its scholarship, its practitioners, and as any teacher of the discipline knows, its students. Rarely a moving speech about journalism is given that does not quote, "The job of the newspaper is to comfort the afflicted and afflict the comfortable."[1] Of course, now there is rarely a speech about journalism that does not quote the prediction from Meyer that the last newspaper will be thrown on its doorstep in 2043. Such was the case when Katharine Weymouth, publisher of the *Washington Post*, CEO of Washington Post Media and granddaughter of Katharine Graham, spoke at Northwestern University's Medill School of Journalism's 2009 convocation. Weymouth's retort: "I've got news for everyone. We're not dead yet." True, but then again Meyer gave newspapers until 2043, and he would be the first to tell you that if his trend line proves true, the end of newspapers will actually be much sooner. No newspaper company will pay the exorbitant costs—salaries and benefits, raw materials, utilities, leases, insurance, taxes—waiting for its last edition to run off the press. Even the Graham family's dear old *Washington Post*, with revenue from its Kaplan test-coaching subsidiary, is not immune.

In fact a January 2010 article on the *Post* in the *New Republic* cited the depth and breadth of the trouble at the newspaper:

> Over the past year, the *Post* has folded its business section into the A-section, killed its book review, revamped its Sunday magazine, and redesigned the entire paper and website, while organizationally merging the print and online editions. Hundreds of staffers have left the *Post* since 2003, thanks to four rounds of buyouts. In 2008, the *Post* began losing money; in 2009, its advertising revenue dropped by $100 million. All of this while the paper was under siege from new competitors, national and local. "The common storyline is the *Post* is flailing," a senior reporter says. "To me, it's slightly different. It's throwing everything up there to see what sticks." "Everybody feels like we're lurching," says another reporter. "A company in chaos" is how a third *Post* staffer describes the state of the paper.[2]

So before the ink stops flowing, what is to be done? Calls for saving journalism have focused on defending it as a community service—a democratic service, and they have come from a variety of sources.

The Newseum, which opened in Washington, D.C., in April 2008 at a cost of $450 million, serves as a 250,000 square-foot homage to the Fourth Estate. At its core is this message: "The free press is a cornerstone of democracy. People have a need to know. Journalists have a right to tell. Finding the facts can be difficult. Reporting the story can be dangerous. Freedom includes the right to be outrageous. Responsibility includes the duty to be fair. News is history in the making. Journalists provide the first draft of history. A free press, at its best, reveals the truth."[3] The 2008–2009 president of the Society of Professional Journalists (SPJ), Dave Aeikens of the *St. Cloud* (Minnesota) *Times*, wrote in his December 2008 column for *Quill*, the organization's magazine:

> The role journalists play in democracy is far too important to give up on it. We chose journalism for a variety of reasons. We like to be in on the action. We like to tell stories, and we like to share with others what is going on and what we have learned. We know that we are the critical link between what is happening in government and the citizens who need that information to make sure it is operating properly. That role will never change.[4]

In a speech she gave at the University of Notre Dame in late 2007, Judy Woodruff of the *NewsHour with Jim Lehrer* on PBS cited what she called "compelling, convincing reasons" journalists are still relevant in a multimedia, multisource news environment. Explained Woodruff: "One is to look at some of the other journalism being practiced these days. Papers like the [New York] *Times* and [Washington] *Post*—and certainly the *Los Angeles Times* even under harrowing conditions—continue to provide a vital public service. There are Tim Russert and Bob Schieffer's Sunday interview shows, the *Economist* magazine, Charlie Rose's public broadcasting program, the foundation that owns and operates the *St. Petersburg* [Florida] *Times*, and much of C-SPAN. These disparate outlets share two common elements: They do good journalism and their reach and influence continue to grow."[5]

The positions of the Newseum founders, the SPJ president, and one of the industry's nameplate journalists are not surprising. They are tried-and-true believers in the social responsibility model of journalism. Trouble is that *surprising* is exactly what the news profession needs right now. It is becoming ever more clear that the same old ways of thinking of journalism as democracy's bedrock are exactly what is wrong with the industry today. Although Woodruff pointed out earlier in her speech that the Tribune Company acquired the *Los Angeles Times*, noting "that few expect that will produce better journalism," her assessment that "reach and influence [will] continue to grow" was even at that time an overstatement. By 2010, for some of the outlets she cited, "reach and influence" proved simply false.

The *Los Angeles Times*, of course, as part of the Tribune Company declared bankruptcy in 2008. Before that, the newsroom staff was cut in half. While the *Washington Post* and the *New York Times* avoided being lumped in with those troubled newspapers at the beginning this crisis, they were not immune. We discussed the *Washington Post*'s fall from grace already. But Michael Wolff, writing for *Vanity Fair*, explained the *Post*'s plummet in a poignant way: "Overnight [in 2007], it goes from an indomitable Washington institution to a hemorrhage of cash."[6] By 2009, the *Washington Post* had cut 900 newsroom jobs, reducing its force to about 500, according to Wolff. The slashes may have been less deep at the *New York Times*, but the paper still has not avoided the axe. In spring 2008, the *New York Times* eliminated 100 newsroom employees, although it added some new jobs during that time. The 2009 picture was much more bleak. In early 2009, the *New York Times* made a temporal 5-percent cut in salaries. By the end of the year, executive editor Bill Keller said it was not enough to avert another round of layoffs, 100 more from the newsroom by the end of 2009.

The other organizations mentioned by Woodruff have faired only slightly better. The *St. Petersburg* (Florida) *Times*, owned by the nonprofit Poynter Institute and often extolled for the virtues of its business model, was still forced to make two major cuts in 2007. The first: a 10-percent decrease in the newsroom staff. The second: a physical shrinking of the newspaper and the news hole. On television, *Meet the Press*, which led the other Sunday morning shows including Schieffer's *Face the Nation* in viewership when Tim Russert was behind the desk, lost its head-of-the-pack status in 2009 when David Gregory took over for Russert who died from a heart attack in 2008. Finally, the proportion of Americans who rely on C-SPAN for information about the presidential campaign remained static, 9 percent in 2000, 8 percent in 2004, and 8 percent in 2008, according to data from the quadrennial survey by the Pew Research Center for the People and the Press and the Pew Internet and American Life Project on campaign news and political communication. At the same time, the percentage of Americans getting campaign news online grew from 9 percent in 2000 to 13 percent in 2004, and 24 percent in 2008.[7] To be fair, Woodruff was not the only one to miss the mark. Many others—journalism practitioners and academics—have predicted a rebound for either the industry or specific news outlets. They have almost universally been wrong.

The fact is that many of the new, so-called innovative efforts being exerted today are still from journalists who were born and bred under the social responsibility of the press model, which is outdated in the current marketplace. The democratic value of newspapers has been recognized in American society as early as the middle of the 19th century by Alexis de Tocqueville who wrote in 1840,

> When no firm and lasting ties any longer unite men, it is impossible to obtain the cooperation of any great number of them unless you can persuade every man whose help is required that he serves his private interests by voluntarily uniting his efforts to those of all the others. That cannot be done habitually and conveniently without the help of a newspaper. Only a newspaper can put the same thought at the same time before a thousand readers. . . . So hardly any democratic association can carry on without a newspaper.[8]

However, this call for a newspaper by de Tocqueville and even the protection afforded by the First Amendment to the Constitution, which was ratified in 1791, did not assert a demand for social responsibility as we understand it today. The press barons of the beginning of the 20th century, for example, operated their newspapers, magazines, radio stations, and wire services with clear political bias attempting to influence elections and legislation.

Social responsibility theory emerged under a confluence of circumstances not the least of which was the public's frustration with the press barons, who saw their power reach even further with the technological advances associated with media during this time. Criticism focused on the press curtailing content to please advertisers, who were becoming ever more important to the business model of news, and the press' attention to the stories of interest and relevance to readers of high socioeconomic status, thereby neglecting in-depth coverage of some important, substantive issues. Upton Sinclair's *The Brass Check* was published in 1920 and served at that time as

the most public indictment of journalism, especially the Associated Press
(AP). Sinclair pinpointed deviant behavior then widespread among the
press including bribery, falsity, and sensationalism. In response, editors
formed the American Society of Newspaper Editors (ASNE) in 1922 and
a year later adopted its *Canons of Journalism*. The organization's first president, Casper Yost of the *St. Louis* (Missouri) *Globe-Democrat*, explained at
its convention in 1923: "General attacks upon the integrity of journalism
as a whole reflect in some measure upon every newspaper and every news-
paperman. In two ways, this Society may counteract the influence of such
antagonism: First, by collective expression, in some form, to show the un-
truth that lies in them, where they are in fact untruthful; and second, by
collective action to establish definite standards of journalistic conduct
which will serve to lessen occasion for truthful criticism."[9] The *Canons*
were adopted in the following days. It is the earliest example of an ethics
code for the industry and set forth appropriate practices relevant to the industry (interdependence and freedom of the press), the journalist (honesty,
accuracy, and impartiality), and the reader (invasion of privacy and public
interest).

Despite early efforts such as these, social responsibility of the press was
really brought to the forefront by the Commission on Freedom of the Press,
also known as the Hutchins Commission, in 1947 when it issued its *Free
and Responsible Press* report. The Hutchins Commission, so named for its
chairman, University of Chicago President Robert Maynard Hutchins, was
formed during World War II by *Time* and *Life* publisher Henry Luce to
determine the proper role of the media in these tumultuous times. The Commission was in large part concerned with the trend of press concentration,
noting that the number of daily newspapers fell to 1,750 in 1945 from a
height of 2,600 in 1909, a 33-percent drop in about 35 years. After four
years of interviews, research, and discussions, the Commission composed
mostly of academics concluded that freedom of the press was in jeopardy
and set forth this gauntlet: "Freedom of the press for the coming period
can only continue as an accountable freedom. Its moral right will be conditioned on its acceptance of this accountability."[10] The American Newspaper Publishers Association (ANPA) saw these calls for accountability
by the Hutchins Commission as an attempt to push government regula-
tions on the media. Yet despite resistance from ANPA and others, the
Commission's approach was accepted in newsrooms nationwide. In fact,
the five functions of a socially responsible press outlined by the Commission have become foundational not only in newsrooms but also in journalism schools. The Commission called on the press to provide a truthful,
comprehensive account of the day's events with context that gives them
meaning; serve as a forum for the exchange of comment and criticism;

offer a representative picture of society; present and clarify goals and values for society; and offer full access to the day's intelligence.[11]

It is from this foundation that the theoretical development of social responsibility of the press emerged. In their seminal book, *Four Theories of the Press,* authors Fred Siebert of Michigan State University, Theodore Peterson of University of Illinois at Urbana-Champaign, and Wilbur Schramm of the East-West Communications Institute established these roots. According to Peterson, who wrote on social responsibility theory, it grew out of a libertarian approach, which lacked any attention to the public's right to know or the ethical responsibilities of journalism. Social responsibility has those principles as essential underpinnings: "Freedom carries concomitant obligations; and the press, which enjoys a privileged position under our government, is obliged to be responsible to society for carrying out certain essential functions of mass communication in contemporary society."[12] Those functions outlined by Peterson differed from those presented by the Hutchins Commission in that they dealt more broadly with the role of the press rather than specific actions required of news outlets. The press under social responsibility theory should be: (1) Serving the political system by providing information, discussion, and debate on public affairs; (2) Enlightening the public so as to make it capable of self-government; (3) Safeguarding the rights of the individual by serving as a watchdog against government; (4) Servicing the economic system, primarily by bringing together the buyers and sellers of goods and services through the medium of advertising; (5) Providing entertainment; and (6) Maintaining its own financial self-sufficiency so as to be free from the pressures of special interests.[13] These obligations have been widely adopted. ASNE (which changed its name to the American Society of News Editors in March 2009), for example, has as key to its *Statement of Principles* this article:

> Responsibility. The primary purpose of gathering and distributing news and opinion is to serve the general welfare by informing the people and enabling them to make judgments on the issues of the time. Newspapermen and women who abuse the power of their professional role for selfish motives or unworthy purposes are faithless to that public trust. The American press was made free not just to inform or just to serve as a forum for debate but also to bring an independent scrutiny to bear on the forces of power in the society, including the conduct of official power at all levels of government.[14]

Journalists took charges such as these seriously, invoking the language of watchdog to explain the purpose of their work.

Therefore, one place to see the enactment of social responsibility theory, or approach as it is sometimes called, is in journalists' professional practices. The fact is that each of the obligations brought up by Peterson addressed journalism content in one fashion or another. The first three demanded quality in-depth reporting on issues related to government and public policy. The fifth, which is also related to editorial content, accounted for lighthearted news, journalism that appeals to a broad base. The fourth element, although focused on advertising, was still content-based and vital to the equation of complete journalistic products. The final point highlighted the financial foundation necessary for unbiased reporting.

However, there is an additional aspect to the content equation not summarized in these duties: content quality, those mechanical values at play in newsrooms that differentiate journalism from other types of information dissemination. Those distinctions between journalism and citizen-produced blogs, glossy lifestyle magazines, or advertorial content have come to be ever more important to journalism in the multiplatform news environment of the 21st century. But what are those specific journalistic values? Here is a provisional list offered by Hodding Carter III, former president and CEO of the John S. and James L. Knight Foundation: depth, multiple sourcing, the layered process of editing and fact checking, professional objectivity, ethical underpinnings, awareness of agenda setting, and community awareness and interest.[15] These values play directly into a vision of a socially responsible press and are the craft of only well-trained, professional reporters and editors. Clearly, investment in authentic, original journalism is at the heart of social responsibility of the press.

Because investment is a key part of the social responsibility equation, a lack of investment from cutbacks and consolidation has drawn the preponderance of attention from journalism practitioners and scholars since the 1990s. Of course, tales of corporate profits pressures are plentiful in the news business today with financial burdens almost universally being cited as responsible for reduced news coverage and quality. Mike Doogan, former metro columnist at the *Anchorage* (Alaska) *Daily News* and now a member of the Alaska House of Representatives, blamed cutbacks as the cause of his unexpected departure from the paper, which is by far the most widely read daily in the state. Of the broader journalism-profit issue, Doogan said, "Newspapers are schizophrenic. The drive to do good journalism and the drive to maximize profits often pull them in completely different directions. Good journalism takes resources. Resources take money. Money spent on journalism doesn't show up on the profit line."[16] Jay Harris, former publisher of Knight Ridder's *San Jose* (California) *Mercury News*, pinpointed the shortsighted profit goals as the impetus behind his sudden, high-profile resignation from the newspaper in 2001.

What troubled me most about the meeting [of *Mercury News* and Knight Ridder executives] was its myopic focus on numbers. It wasn't the cutting so much. I have cut and forced others to over many years. I was taught how to do so by the best on both sides of the table. What troubled me—something that had never happened to me before in all my years in the company—was that little or no attention was paid to the consequences of achieving 'the number.' There was virtually no discussion of the damage that would be done to the quality and aspirations of the *Mercury News* as a journalistic endeavor or to its ability to fulfill its responsibilities to the community.[17]

Early concerns expressed by Doogan, Harris, and others found traction as demands from Wall Street for wide profit margins increased and the trend of media consolidation corporatized even more news outlets.

The Project for Excellence in Journalism's 2006 report of its ongoing study, the *State of the News Media,* detailed the impact of consolidation. At that time 20 newspaper companies owned about 40 percent of the nation's newspapers, which accounted for nearly 70 percent of daily circulation. The top 10 newspaper companies accounted for more than 50 percent of daily circulation alone. Specifically, in addition to the nation's largest circulation newspaper—*USA Today*—Gannett, the nation's largest newspaper company, also owned about 90 other newspaper properties and more than 20 television news stations. In 2006, the McClatchy Company announced a deal to buy Knight Ridder's newspaper holdings for $4.5 billion in cash and stock, plus the assumption of $2 billion in debt. McClatchy immediately announced the sale of 12 of those Knight Ridder properties, retaining 20 dailies, several nondailies, and 10 foreign new bureaus. With this, McClatchy became the country's second-largest newspaper publisher. McClatchy sold the Minneapolis *Star Tribune* in 2007, dropping it to the third-largest newspaper company behind the Tribune and Gannett companies. The ownership consolidation trend, however, was not confined to newspaper-dominated companies. In 2005, five corporations controlled the majority of the big news brands in the United States. Take these two examples. News Corporation, owned by Rupert Murdoch, had FOX, Harper-Collins, the *New York Post,* the *Weekly Standard, TV Guide,* DirecTV, and 35 television stations. General Electric dominated with NBC, CNBC, MSNBC, Telemundo, Bravo, Universal Pictures, and 28 television stations. Of course, ownership status is almost constantly in flux. Since 2005, for instance, News Corporation has purchased the *Wall Street Journal* and spun off an exclusively business network from the FOX channel.[18]

Parts of the news business, newspapers especially, have been so plagued by falling advertising revenues and readership figures that the trend of corporatization has stalled as of late. As an alternative, there seems to be interest in returning some newspapers to private ownership. A group of local investors has publically expressed interest in buying the Tribune-owned *Baltimore Sun* since 2006. Entertainment executive David Geffen offered

$2 billion for the *Los Angeles Times* before it was sold under the Tribune Company umbrella to Sam Zell in 2007. Two years later Geffen also made a failed play for a nearly 20-percent stake in the New York Times Company, which also turned down a 2006 offer to buy the *Boston Globe* from Jack Welch, former chief of General Electric, and advertising executive Jack Connors. There has been at least one public to private sale of note. In 2006, Philadelphia Media Holdings led by Brian Tierney, a public relations executive, bought the *Philadelphia Inquirer* and the *Philadelphia Daily News* when the McClatchy Company purchased the papers in its acquisition of Knight Ridder. By 2009, however, Philadelphia Media Holdings had filed for bankruptcy. Still, the hope for private ownership is that it gives news outlets enough breathing room from pressing Wall Street profit concerns to return to the socially responsible reporting for which these newspapers became known. For now, the focus remains on the implications of the corporatization movement on news content and its quality, necessary elements of a socially responsible press. Media economist Robert Picard summarized, "Economic pressures are becoming the primary focus shaping the behavior of American newspaper companies."[19] The argument is that consolidation and corporate ownership have forced at least two troubling results: reduced the quantity and quality of community coverage, and increased bias in reporting by some media outlets of their parent companies.

Changes in community coverage have ultimately come about as a result of layoffs and cutbacks in reporting budgets, which have had an immediate and real impact on local news. Simply put, with fewer feet on the ground reporting, news outlets are forced to cover their communities in new ways. To compensate for fewer locally produced stories, editors and producers have become reliant on alternative sources of news. Although these substitute approaches may vary by medium, some are particularly troubling. Chain-owned outlets typically have access to stories from papers and stations across their companies, often utilizing not only other papers' nonlocal features but also their evergreen content, those stories that never go out of season. Evergreen pieces do not have a news peg and are typically lighthearted features. Examples include a story on how to decorate your nursery (or any other room for that matter), an article on compounding bank interest and the value of investing early in your life, and a piece on a particular hobby such as knitting. In addition to use of company-specific content, across the board, there has been increasing reliance on wire service stories. This is especially true in the cases of news outlets, such as Cox Newspapers and Media General, that have cut bureaus in Washington, D.C. Finally, in the strained news environment that requires reporters to produce more content for more channels of distribution with fewer resources, there has been an increased likelihood of what can be called "behind-the-desk reporting" marked by an overreliance on print and video news releases and easily accessed sources. The ultimate result is a deterioration of a strong local news agenda.

In addition, some have argued that corporatization has led to reduced autonomy in reporting by news outlets on their parent companies. CNBC has been criticized for a conflict of interest in its reporting of the financial markets, its mainstay, because its parent company, General Electric, has Jeffrey Immelt as its chairman and chief executive officer. Immelt is on the board of the Federal Reserve Bank of New York. The *Wall Street Journal* has had increasing accusations of right-wing bias since it was purchased by Murdoch's News Corporation, which also owns the FOX News cable network. And Howard Kurtz, a *Washington Post* media columnist, has been pinpointed as failing to disclose his financial relationship with CNN, where he has his own show, in newspaper columns about the network, its shows, and its personalities.

The weakening foundation of social responsibility of the press has elicited two primary reactions. First, perhaps to be expected, there has been a call for the expansion of social responsibility, charging that news organizations should engage the public, not just inform them. These beliefs and related efforts have taken form as the public journalism movement. Second, there have been concerted efforts to establish socially responsible actions as smart business investments. That is, if you cannot appeal to publishers' and owners' sense of responsibility, appeal to their pocketbooks instead.

Davis "Buzz" Merritt, former editor of the *Wichita* (Kansas) *Eagle* and author of *Knightfall: Knight Ridder and How the Erosion of Newspaper Journalism Is Putting Democracy at Risk*, and New York University's Jay Rosen, former director of the Kettering Foundation's Project on Public Life and the Press, brought forth the concept of public journalism. The idea is that the work of journalists should extend beyond news production and dissemination to concerted and focused efforts to engage their readers—and even nonreaders—in public life. Public journalism, according to the two, extended the theory of social responsibility of the press to demand of the institution that it *encourage* civic engagement. Rosen explained,

> What becomes of the press when the public's constitution alters or weakens? Some journalists were discovering what happens: a public was not always there for them to inform, a troubling development that caused them to think hard about what they were doing and why. The more I grasped this, the more it involved me with people who were beginning to wrestle with some difficult problems: fewer readers for their best work, a rising disgust with politics and journalism, and a growing feeling that the craft was misfiring as it attempted to interest people in the news of the day. Eventually, I came to

the conclusion that a better way to "do" ideas about the press was to interest the press in the germ of an idea: that journalism's purpose was to see the public into fuller existence. Informing people followed from that.[20]

Merritt spearheaded public journalism efforts at the *Wichita Eagle* in the early 1990s. He ran a series of projects for the community's voters. Surveys conducted by the *Eagle* identified the issues important to local voters including education, taxes, and economic development. Then in the 1991 local election, the newspaper targeted candidates with questions on their related policies. The *Eagle* also ran extensive issue-oriented coverage, as opposed to what is called horse-race coverage, an appropriate analogy for stories focused on who is in the moment-by-moment lead in the polls. The newspaper even ran blank space—a bold decision for an outlet accustomed to using every inch of space for editorial or advertising content—when candidates refused to state their policies. Voting was also promoted in newspaper advertisements and a voting guide. Then in 1992, the *Eagle* launched *The People Project: Solving It Ourselves*, a series of articles on local issues identified via almost 200 in-depth interviews with community members. There was particular attention to solution to problems and opportunities for citizens to become involved.

With activities such as these at its roots since its inception, the public journalism movement has drawn ample debate with supporters advocating community involvement, and detractors saying it either overstretches the bounds of the social responsibility of the press or is ineffective. Although the conversation is less robust now, the public journalism movement posited an important marker in the history of social responsibility of the press extending that there is a responsibility to not only inform the community but inspire it to action. While some continue to disagree that this was an appropriate extension of the social responsibility of the press, there is no doubt that the pubic journalism movement brought the connection between social responsibility of the press and democracy to the forefront.

Belief in the necessity of a socially responsible press to a healthy democracy led to another line of thought, the idea that being socially responsible can be profitable. UNC-Chapel Hill's Meyer has been one of the most vocal proponents of this perspective. His most recent book, *The Vanishing Newspaper: Saving Journalism in the Information Age*, established quantitative evidence of a positive relationship between daily readership and a newspaper's quality as defined by its credibility, reporting and editing accuracy, readability, and editorial vigor. Although the specific metrics related to these variables are not in and of themselves measures of social responsibility, they are clearly closely related. Meyer's argument is that in Jurgensmeyer's influence model of journalism, the idea that the social influence of newspapers is essential output is based in part on the quality of a newspaper's mechanics.

Meyer's concern is that commercial newspapers are simply too entrenched in quality-trimming decisions, which he likens to a "harvesting strategy."[21] Meyer explained, "A stagnant industry's position is harvested by raising prices and lowering quality, trusting that customers will continue to be attracted by the brand name rather than the substance for which the brand once stood. Eventually, of course, they will wake up. But as the harvest metaphor implies, this is a nonrenewable, take-the-money-and-run strategy. Once harvested, the market position is gone."[22] As people turn to new sources of news or from news altogether, there is concern that Meyer's fears have been realized.

Even within the environment rife with economic pressures on journalism, a small subset of outlets within the larger news journalism context allows practical insight on the quality-cost equation. These newspapers and news stations supported either by foundations, trusts, or consumer and tax dollars, are at least partially protected from the advertising-driven marketplace and are therefore noticeably focused on the public interest. Some of them are well known for their clout, including National Public Radio (NPR), the *St. Petersburg Times* (a for-profit newspaper owned by the nonprofit Poynter Institute), *Mother Jones*, *Harper's* magazine, *Consumer Reports*, and *National Geographic*. Others operate quietly in their communities, such as *Pacifica Radio* that started in Berkeley, California, but now has sister stations in Houston, Los Angeles, New York, and Washington, D.C.; the *New London* (Connecticut) *Day*; the *Manchester* (New Hampshire) *Union Leader*; and the *Anniston* (Alabama) *Star*. Although the business models of these newspapers, magazines, and stations vary widely, what is clear is that the noncommercial model means less attention to extracting wide profit margins, which we have seen among commercial news outlets. That is, while the editors and publishers of the noncommercial entities are still careful to point out that they do have financial responsibilities to stay solvent, there are advantages. University of Maryland's Carl Sessions Stepp, a senior editor of *American Journalism Review*, explained, "Less-commercial media can think more in terms of social responsibility, with less oppression from short-term profit demands."[23] Stepp argued that said freedom has a discernible impact on news content, citing more coverage of international affairs and government and less coverage of celebrities, fluff, and "pizzazz."

In fact, the benefits of noncommercial management have been so widely recognized that nonprofit business models are drawing the preponderance of attention in conversations about the future of the news business. Charles Lewis, a former producer at CBS News' *60 Minutes* and founder of the Center for Public Integrity, has been a charismatic proponent. "These new and future nonprofit institutions could be ways to rejuvenate and sustain the soul of journalism," he wrote in a 2007 *Columbia Journalism Review* article promoting a noncommercial approach to news.[24] Other supporters include Downie and Schudson in their report *The Reconstruction of American Journalism* and Robert McChesney and John Nichols in their 2010 book from Nation Books, *The Death and Life of American Journalism*. In fact, Senator Benjamin Cardin of Maryland introduced legislation in 2009 that would allow newspapers to become nonprofits as a means of survival.

The 2009 Senate hearing on the Future of Journalism and Newspapers is only further evidence that concern about the business of journalism is widespread. Senator John Kerry, chairman of the Commerce Subcommittee on Communications and Technology, in his opening remarks, summarized:

> A brass plaque on a wall at Columbia University's School of Journalism bears the words of the legendary newspaper publisher Joseph Pulitzer: "Our Republic and its press will rise and fall together." If we take seriously this notion that the press is the Fourth Estate, or the fourth branch of government, then we need to examine the future of journalism in the digital information age, what it means to our Republic, and to our democracy. Americans once counted on newspapers to be the rock on which journalism, the best sense of the word journalism, was based. As Princeton University communications professor Paul Starr notes in this most recent edition of *Columbia Journalism Review*, "More than any other medium, newspapers have been the eyes on the state, our check on private abuses, our civic alarm systems." Most of us in this room probably begin our day still with a newspaper, maybe two or three. Newspapers have been a part of our daily lives since we were old enough to read and we learned about our neighborhoods, and our countries, and our world from newspapers. They entertained us, sometimes they enraged us but always they informed us. Today it's fair to say newspapers look like an endangered species and many people in the industry and outside of it are so writing. . . . We're here to talk not only about the conditions that led to these jolting statistics but about what they mean to us, what they may mean to a country that appears to be reading less or that finds information in snippets rather than whole pieces. We need to understand what it means about news delivery during a time of great creative turmoil and transition within the market for news delivery and how we might preserve the core societal function that is served by an independent and diverse news media.[25]

But what was most alarming about the hearing was its lead participant. Marissa Mayer, vice president of Search Products and User Experience, was the first to testify. Notably, she is also the co-chair of the Knight Commission on the Information Needs of Communities in a Democracy.[26] There is no doubt that Mayer's voice is an essential one in the larger conversation about the future of news. She is bright, innovative, and affiliated with one of the clear game-changers in the media world, Google. The trouble comes in that journalists have had to concede to nonjournalists when it comes to the future of news as it relates to the audience. This reveals the primary weakness of the social responsibility model of journalism. It is consumed by serving the whole at the expense of its parts—the people.

Most journalists are too consumed by the *idea* of service to be lending any real attention to if they are even providing a service anymore. While it can be argued that stories are important even if they go unread or unheard because they hold the powers that be in check, it is unlikely that journalists want to trace this argument to its end line: reporting and writing or producing for no audience whatsoever. We are, of course, on this path already. News outlets recognized for excelling in their social responsibility are no longer guaranteed enough of an audience or an associated business model for success. The *Rocky Mountain News* in Denver, Colorado, was lauded in 2008 for a six-month investigation that uncovered the Department of Labor's deliberate denial of appropriate compensation due to former nuclear weapons workers. The *Rocky Mountain News* closed in 2009.

Now, in this environment where discussions of the need for a socially responsible press continue to bubble to the surface, there has also been a concerted effort to experiment on the part of news outlets hoping to avoid the *Rocky*'s fate. Let us be clear that in the name of being socially responsible, much of this work has been aimed simply and squarely at preserving the old way of doing things. For example, in August 2009 the *Philadelphia Inquirer* announced a new policy that investigative, enterprise, trend, and news feature stories would be published in print first and then on the Web. Although the *Inquirer* amended its plan to simultaneous print-online release, this decision reflects a protectionist philosophy, trying to push readers to the newspaper because print advertising revenue still trumps online advertising revenue by 10 times and often more. The underlying philosophy of efforts such as these is that good, socially responsible journalism is expensive and to retain product quality, newspaper companies have to find ways to sell more papers thereby shoring up revenue streams.

At the same time, news outlets have been looking for alternative sources of meaningful revenue. An October 2009 e-mail advertisement from the *New York Times* to former subscribers to the paper offered a bundle deal, a one-year *Times* Kindle-edition subscription with the Kindle DX and a cover, for $499. The offer essentially gave the subscription away for free. But assuming a healthy partnership with Amazon.com, the *Times* could draw some initial revenue, year-long commitments, and the opportunity for renewals. In addition, the *Times* announced in January 2010 that it would charge frequent users of its Web site for access. While the definition of "frequent" seems to be undetermined at this time—the *Times* does not plan to hit the pay-for-access switch until 2011—the position is clear: It needs revenue. To this end, the *Times* has also tried nonnews alternatives. In August 2009, it launched a wine club. Although unaffiliated with the newspaper and its well-known critics, the wine club invites members to order packages at different price points, which will be shipped along with wine, food, and travel content from the *Times* archives.

Other efforts by news companies have been directly related to content and most of these have been hyperlocal. The *East Valley Tribune* in Mesa, Arizona, doubled its zoning in 2007. Before then, it had two editions, one for Phoenix's growing eastern suburbs and the other for the affluent Scottsdale area. Since then: one for the town of Gilbert, which grew from 25,000 to about 200,000 residents in 15 years; one for the SanTan region, including Queen Creek and parts of Pinal County; one for the core of the East Valley, which includes Mesa, Chandler, and Tempe; and still one for Scottsdale.

All of these examples represent new ways of doing things, but they are all hindered by an old way of thinking, the social responsibility model. There has been absolutely no effort by journalists to redefine the role of their work outside of this dated model. The important question today is not: "How do journalists serve their communities?" The essential question is: "What is the real job that democracy requires of journalists?" The real job today is reaching an audience, even if it is a select one, and compelling members of that audience to care about issues and people that they otherwise might not have known. The key news value is relevance. Not enough people currently care about general-circulation news for it to present a sustainable model for the future of journalism.

But for news to be truly relevant to its audience, journalists have to conquer the task of understanding their readers, listeners, and users with a depth that was not required previously. This must go leaps beyond the scant attention being provided to the audience now vis-à-vis news operations' marketing departments and external reports from the Audit Bureau of Circulations (ABC), the Nielsen Company, Mediamark Research (MRI), or online measurement devices. These current efforts are too shallow and misfocused. They are either aimed at selling the product as it is, or counting the people and the characteristics of those who are still buying.

There are many ideas being batted around about what the future of the news should look like. Too many of them are consumed by new business models for doing the work that has always been done even if that work is irrelevant in the current marketplace. They rarely deal with the audience in any meaningful way. Further, most of these conversations conflate journalism and journalistic entities, something that should be avoided. Saving news does not mean saving newspapers, saving the *Washington Post*, saving the Tribune Company, or saving ABC News. Remember it is the old ways of thinking that in part caused the problems of today. All we have done is left old media leaders floundering in a new media world. Many of the conversations about the future of journalism exemplify this. For example, an article in the 2007 issue of the *Journalist*, the magazine of the Society of Professional Journalists (SPJ), highlights seven ways media organizations can succeed in a multimedia environment: own breaking news; invest in hyperlocal content; embrace databases that can be searched by users online; use multimedia features; gather evergreen content; maximize content across devices (the Web, e-mail, mobile devices); and make newspapers a dialog by allowing readers to post comments to stories, contact reporters, and post their own content. Written by Rob Curley, then vice president of product development at Washingtonpost-Newsweek Interactive and now editor of the new media division of the *Las Vegas Sun* and the Greenspun Media Group, the article makes minimal mention of the audience while purporting "what matters most is that the trusted relationship with our audience survives."[27] Agreed. But social responsibility theory is no longer at the crux of that relationship.

Social responsibility theory has a strong history in journalism and mass communication scholarship but has drawn attention as of late due to increasing concentration of ownership within the news industry. The corporatization of media and deterioration of newspapers has exacerbated concerns that journalists are not attending to the people that should, according to social responsibility theory, be their first concerns—the citizens in lieu of short-term profit pressures. The audience is paramount. Journalists today are engaged in a battle to save, to serve, democracy. It is a bit like tilting at windmills. The real battle will be won person by person based on a new model of service—the identity-based model of journalism.

PART TWO

The Individual Is Very Much Alive

CHAPTER 3

Audience Needs
and Actions

It is what you read when you don't have to that determines what
you will be when you can't help it.
—Oscar Wilde

We actually know a great deal about who reads what and why. Understanding this context is part of developing a new audience-oriented or identity-based model of journalism. It requires a deep look at what researchers call *uses and gratifications*. It is important to note at the outset of this discussion that scholarly debate surrounds the efficacy of uses and gratifications as a mass communication theory. Specifically, detractors assert that a true theory must predict or explain a relationship between or among variables. The uses and gratifications approach simply asserts that individuals use the mass media to gratify their needs, and it stakes its strength in its ability to allow the study of individual psychological desires and motives across channels and content. The underlying premise of the uses and gratifications model is an active audience composed of self-aware, message-seeking, message-selecting individuals.

From its inception the uses and gratifications model—a description that is more appropriate than calling it a theory—has relied on the active-audience assumption; that is, that people are deliberate and discriminating in making their media choices. The principal power then rests with the audience, where individuals define their needs and take control of the media-seeking process in an attempt to gratify those needs. Such an approach suggests that media are relegated to serving the audience and thereby competing among one another for attention. This, by the way, should have been our first hint that journalists would be less than interested in considering this perspective. Still, an important intellectual contribution made by uses and gratifications research was that it established individuals' social and psychological needs as integral in shaping their media use.

The innovative individual focus of uses and gratifications was one of the first among media effect theories to assume an active audience. In fact, the uses and gratifications approach—utilized by Herta Herzog in her groundbreaking research on housewives and radio soap operas, and Paul Lazarsfeld and Frank Stanton in their expansive attention to radio—added an audience-centered line of research to the discipline, which had previously been exclusively source-dominated.[1] Lazarsfeld, a renowned sociologist and founder of the Bureau for Applied Social Research at Columbia University, and Stanton, a media executive at CBS and eventually its president for 25 years, developed a device during this time nicknamed by the network "Little Annie." The value of Little Annie was that it tracked the reactions of a room full of people to media content. At regular intervals, the audience was prompted by an indicator light to express their "likes" or "dislikes" by hitting a green or red button. Little Annie was really the first example of the technology that television stations use today to trace the moment-by-moment reactions from a select group of respondents—Republicans, Democrats, and undecided voters—in U.S. presidential debates. Little Annie was used by Lazarsfeld and Stanton to determine audience interest in new programming and establish a general understanding of what attracts individuals to media content. Although eventually a huge amount of data was drawn from this line of research, one important generalization was reported on in a 1942 issue of *Time* magazine: "Many a listener likes or dislikes programs or passages for reasons all his own."[2] This perspective suggested that inherent needs motivated individuals' searches for gratifications via media use, thereby establishing the idea that while audiences collectively seek gratifications, individuals use and react to media differently. Which means uses and gratifications are not universal.

Despite the recognition of individualism in uses and gratifications research, the preponderance of early studies sought to identify broad audience motives, with each listing functions served by the content of the medium and then categorizing them. This, of course, paralleled the media industry's goal of attracting a mass audience. Herzog, for example, focused her early research on housewives' attraction to radio soap operas, eventually detecting three primary gratifications: emotional release, a venue for wishful thinking, and advice. Katherine Wolf and Marjorie Fiske, also of Lazarsfeld's Bureau for Applied Social Research, found similar gratifications in their evaluation of children and comics.[3] Specifically, they determined that children read comics to explore a fantasy world, for absorption or escape, and for relaxation. Using similar methods, Bernard Berelson, also at the Bureau for a short time, turned attention to newspapers during the 1945 New York City delivery-person strike—no better time to study what people care about in a product when they do not have access to it—and found that the gratifications differed.[4] According to Berelson, people used the newspapers for information about and interpretation of public affairs, as a tool for daily living, for social prestige, and for social contact. Methodological and conceptual shortcomings of this early work were noted, with particular attention to the shallow study of the gratifications themselves. At the time, researchers qualitatively outlined gratifications. They did not quantitatively examine the nature of the gratifications or the potential relationships among them.

The next generation of uses and gratifications research, however, expanded attention to determining the variables—social and psychological—that led to different gratification typologies. Attention to these deeper variables coincided with both the penetration of television into American households, as well as disruptive social changes including racial tension, war protests, and increased crime. Notably, the preponderance of uses and gratifications studies during this time attended to television, but the fundamental impetus was not the medium, the focus remained on the individual. Mental ability, social relationships, mood, and race all became important contexts for uses and gratifications research during this time.

The real paradigm shift presented by uses and gratifications, however, did not take firm hold until the 1970s, mirroring the psychological changes in society that also focused on the self. A team of researchers at the Hebrew University of Jerusalem and the Israel Institute of Applied Social Research (later named the Guttman Institute and then closed in 1996) synthesized a typology of the audience's uses, and social and psychological gratifications.[5] They specifically explored the impact of media—newspaper, television, radio, cinema, and books—consumption in Israel and ultimately suggested three empirical clusters of needs. First, people have needs associated with the strengthening or weakening of their contact experiences. Second, those contact experiences can be cognitive, affective, or integrative. And third, the contact experiences are with some referent such as the self, friends, family, or political or social institution. In this early work the researchers concluded that "the centrality of the newspaper for knowledge and integration in the socio-political arena cannot be overstated."[6] Although these findings were based in Israel, there was reason to believe the results were relevant in the United States as well. The newspaper was still a dominant medium in the early 1970s. Remember that in 1970, more than three-quarters of adults read a newspaper on an average weekday. As such, research began in the

1980s and continued through the early part of the 21st century that focused specifically on the uses and gratifications of the American newspaper.

The preponderance of uses and gratifications research during this time was focused on key demographic and sociologic areas. This charge was in part led by Leo Bogart, now well known for his book *Press and Public: Who Reads What, When, Where, and Why in American Newspapers*, an extensive summary of readership studies done since 1960 under his direction at the Newspaper Advertising Bureau (which merged with five organizations into the Newspaper Association of America [NAA] in 1992).[7] Citing historical social trends impacting readership, including the reduction in leisure time and the changing nature of the metropolis, Bogart traced the evolution of reading habits with direct attention to the lagging motivation to read. Researchers have followed this lead with studies on more specific populations such as young adults. For example, a 1996 study of leisure time and leisure reading among college students concluded that television is considered by this audience to be entertainment, and that reading print-based media is considered to be work.[8] Then research done in 2003 found relationships between college student newspaper readership and several variables: length of time at the university, hours spent on campus, participation in campus activities, and friendships. Increased attachment—physical or emotional—to a campus correlated with increased readership.[9] The challenge presented by these findings is that they generally "blamed" societal factors for individuals' abandonment of news.

But a subset of uses and gratifications work examined the unique traits of the medium—at the time, newspapers—as potential elements of gratification. For example, a survey of students at California State University-Chico revealed important differences between the audience's interest in the campus weekly and a local community weekly, as well as their disinterest in the local community daily.[10] The daily, the researchers asserted, was too heavy on government-meeting stories at the expense of more interesting, issue-orientated stories. Further, the daily lacked events listings and coverage of leisure topics, but it was still 35 cents daily (75 cents on Sunday) compared to the weeklies, which were free. In later research Christopher Beaudoin, now of Texas A&M University but at Indiana University at the time of this work, along with Esther Thorson of the University of Missouri found a key factor related to news use to be credibility, which they operationalized as perceptions of accuracy and fairness in media coverage of specified groups classified by race, age, socioeconomic status, and sexual preference.[11] The crucial value of this medium-based approach was that it suggested that efforts could be made to alter media products to positively influence usage.

In the academy, this attention to the role of the medium led to the development of the idea of media substitution. Fundamentally, this established what we now know to be absolutely true: *People view different media as inter-changeable in providing gratifications*. This does not mean they see media as exactly the same, but rather that there are many "good enough" substitutions. Media substitution research has blossomed with the modern expansion of the media landscape. Willingness of consumers to utilize substitute products, which in the case of daily newspaper include print, online, broadcast, and the most recent entrant mobile media, has clearly indicated an elastic demand.

Probably because this media substitution phenomenon is present among today's young adults, they have been the subjects of the preponderance of current research on media usage. In 2007, a team from the University of North Texas relied on a uses and gratifications framework to study new media adoption among young adults as it relates to terrestrial radio.[12] At that time, the team determined that the audience owned and used a fair amount of technology for the time. More than 98 percent owned a personal computer (this was a sample of college students), 81 percent had a cable or satellite connection to the Internet, 61 percent had a mobile phone, and 58 percent had an MP3 player. While 88 percent listened to AM/FM radio, it fell short of MP3 technology on all but one gratification, being a source of news and information. MP3's gratifications: provided a variety of listening choices, helped them pass the time, gave them greater control over the listening experience, helped them relax, provided music and entertainment when it was convenient for them, helped them forget about their daily chores, gave them a number of different entertainment choices, helped them occupy their time, and gave them the best value for their money. In part, these gratifications explain why we see so many college students with buds in their ears walking to classes these days.

But attention turned to this audience long before iPods, Facebook, and Twitter. In the mid-1970s two professors from the University of Oklahoma in Norman, Ernest Larkin and Gerald Grotta, were some of the first who attempted to unearth young adults' wants, needs, and desires associated with news.[13] Because of the timing of their work, they focused on newspapers in comparison to televisions, magazines, and radio in a two-step method. First, in a series of focus group interviews Larkin and Grotta sought insights into media attitudes and uses. Second, they utilized that information to develop a thorough questionnaire, which was administered to 500 randomly selected subjects between 19 and 34 years old. The researchers detected a more favorable perception of television than newspapers where broadcast was identified as a vehicle of entertainment—but also as the most accurate, most informative, most ethical, easiest to use, and most essential of the four media types. Respondents tended, in contrast, to see print as an information-gathering tool. And although there was no sense of active distaste for newspapers, respondents were generally apathetic. They indicated that the usefulness of a daily newspaper was in its application to daily living as a consumer guide with how-to guides, best buys, and advertising. Since these early findings, there has been continued attention to the young adult audience.

Expounding on the meaning of the newspaper to young adults, or more specifically the uses and gratifications of the medium, Kevin Barnhurst, currently of the University of Illinois-Chicago, and Ellen Wartella, now of Northwestern University, engaged in what can be called a life-history methodology, gathering and evaluating autobiographical narratives from participants.[14] The approach was constructed to track the development of readership habits across time. It is important to note that during this time, the early 1990s, news executives firmly believed that young adults would "age into" their products as they began to pay tax, buy homes, and have children in public schools. We know now that the news executives were very mistaken. Even then, Barnhurst and Wartella found that while young adults related to the newspaper as a ritual, a symbol, and a tool, they also detected an important gap: Young adults "consider the facts in newspapers boring because they deal with contexts unrelated to their lives."[15] Newspaper readership, once an institutionalized behavior of the American family, was already being discarded at this time—namely by the young adult audience Barnhurst and Wartella studied. The weekday newspaper readership for 18- to 24-year-olds tumbled each decade: from 73 percent in 1970, to 59 percent in 1980, to 53 percent in 1990, to 40 percent in 2000, to 34 percent in the year-end data from 2007, according to aggregate data from NAA.[16] Readership statistics for 25- to 34-year-olds were no more uplifting: 77 percent in 1970, 62 percent in 1980, 58 percent in 1990, 41 percent in 2000, and 34 percent in 2007. The combination of Barnhurst and Wartella's findings and the NAA data of declining readership were supported by the uses and gratifications model. The young adult audience, in general, found no useful value in newspapers. Paying taxes, buying a home, and having children did not change this perspective.

Perhaps as a result of this, some of the uses and gratifications research focused on this audience began to stray away from news to evaluate more entertainment-based media. Researchers at Kent State University attempted to add richness to the uses and gratifications literature by studying the meanings that people have for a source of communication, which in this case was popular music.[17] Other sources that were examined: movies,[18] the Internet,[19] social networking Web sites such as Facebook and MySpace,[20] YouTube,[21] and competition-based reality television including the *Apprentice* and *Survivor*.[22] In addition, research done by Richard Vincent of Indiana State University and Michael Basil of the University of Lethbridge in

Canada tied together the work on information- and entertainment-based media and young adults.[23] Focusing on a college-age audience, Vincent and Basil developed a four-part typology of media uses and gratifications sought. The elements of the key constructs—surveillance, escape, boredom, and entertainment—are detailed in Figure 3.1.

Surveillance	So I can understand the world
	To find out things I need to know about daily life
	It makes me want to learn more about things
	Because it helps me learn things about myself and others
	It shows me what society is like nowadays
	So I can learn about what might happen to me
	It help me judge what political leaders are really like
	So I can keep up with what the government is doing
	So I can talk with other people about what's covered
	It helps me satisfy by curiosity
	So I can learn what is going on in the country and the world
Escape	It helps me get away from everyday worries
	It helps me when I want to be cheered up
	It helps me forget about school and homework
	It helps me take my mind off things
	It helps me relax
Boredom	When I have nothing better to do
	Just because it's on
	Because it passes the time, especially when I'm bored
	When there's no one else to talk to or be with
	Because it's a good thing to turn on when I'm alone
Entertainment	Because it's entertaining
	Because it's enjoyable
	Because it's exciting
	Because it's thrilling
	Because it amuses me
	It sometimes gives me a good laugh or cry

Figure 3.1: Vincent and Basil's typology of media uses and gratifications among college students

Vincent and Basil found the surveillance gratification to be a significant predictor of all news media use. This was not surprising since surveillance was associated with learning and knowledge, the consistent strengths of the news media throughout uses and gratifications research. Escape, Vincent and Basil determined, was not a significant predictor of print news use; boredom showed a negative relationship with newsmagazine use; and entertainment had a positive relationship with both cable and local television news viewing. Again, no surprises.

But for all that we know about uses and gratifications from scholarly research, there has been minimal attention to these concepts in professional news production and dissemination practices. This is even true in the news industry's efforts to attract young adults via new products and personalities. The relationship between the academy and the media has been so weak that even directly applicable lessons went unlearned or even ignored throughout most news outlets nationwide. Barnhurst and Wartella knew that young adults were disinterested in newspapers in the early 1990s, which sadly was years before the industry came to this recognition in any genuine way.

Some current research is bridging the academic-industry gap. From 2001 to 2004, Northwestern University's Media Management Center (MMC) and the associated Readership Institute (RI) undertook an expansive study to determine the experiences that cause people to engage with or disengage from print media. In 2005 they expanded their attention to online media. Over the course of their multiyear study, researchers were able to determine the experiences—or uses—that motivated or inhibited the consumption of media based on type, as well as the potential strength of a singular experience based on the time, completeness, and frequency of readership or use. Although not conceptualized by the MMC/RI as an offshoot of uses and gratifications, this work really marked the model's advancement. As such, it is worth a detailed review.

The MMC/RI conceptualized an experience with a media outlet as a construct composed of the brand perception of that media entity, which was based on its news and advertising content and its service excellence. Even at the outset of this work, the MCC/RI noted that news and advertising content and service excellence have direct effects on readership as well, but the research instead dealt with the effect on readership as mediated by brand perception. In addition to that intellectual advancement, much of the value of the MMC/RI's work was its scale. There was an initial qualitative stage, implemented in 2001 and 2002, in which researchers conducted one-on-one interviews with light and heavy newspaper readers. That phase produced 275 qualitative statements regarding how respondents felt about and reacted to their local daily newspapers. Then to determine the presence and strength of these experiences in the larger marketplace, the MCC/RI conducted a mail survey of 10,000 people who were at least light readers of their local dailies. The resulting *Newspaper Experience Study* led to the establishment of 44 experiences that individuals have with newspapers.[24] Specifically, there were 26 motivators, associated with increasing newspaper readership, and 18 inhibitors, associated with decreasing newspaper readership. They are outlined in Figure 3.2.

Motivators	Inhibitors
It is a regular part of my day	It wastes my time
It looks out for my interest	I only scan the headlines
It gives me something to talk about	It is too much for me; I feel like I'm drowning in news
It makes me smarter	It lacks a distinctive personality
It tells me about people I know	It is too much (too many pages, stories too long)
It touches and inspires me	It is awkward to handle
It has high-quality, unique content	It lacks a local focus
I connect with the writers	I enjoy reading it on the Web
Reading it is my personal timeout	I get poor service
It makes me more interesting	It has unappealing stories
It commands my attention	It has a gender bias
It tells all sides of the story	I do not like sharing it
It shows me diversity	The advertisements are annoying or unimpressive
It takes a stand	I prefer to media multitask
It is my "dining companion"	The advertisements are uninformative
It turns me on with surprise and humor	It is politically biased
I clip and save stories	It makes me anxious
It grabs me visually	I critique it as I read
It makes me want to read	
I pass it around to others	
The advertisements have credibility	
It give me value for my money	
I can pick it up or take it with me	
It guides me	
I am a news junkie	
The advertisements are useful	

Figure 3.2: Motivators and inhibitors of newspaper readership developed by the Media Management Center and the Readership Institute

Since this early work, the MCC/RI has expanded its experience work in several relevant dimensions. The primary track for this research has been attention to the infrequent or light reader. A 2004 report attempted to warn newspapers of what lay ahead: "Newspapers that want to forge strong bonds with younger and more diverse readers must prepare themselves for nothing short of revolution."[25] It recommended that newspapers innovate on several key experiences for their readers: give them something to talk about; make them smarter; look out for their civic and personal interests; provide them good service; do not give them too much; give them value for their money; include useful advertisements; and do not discriminate or stereotype. To show evidence of the need for revolution, the RI partnered with the Minneapolis *Star Tribune* in 2005 to test different version of the paper's front page with what was then considered the elusive young reader.[26] In fact, this project led to the recommendation that newspapers must "edit for experiences," and that the story selection and presentation styles used on the front page have a significant impact on drawing young reader interest. According to the authors, John Lavine and Mary Nesbitt, now dean and associate dean, respectively, of the Medill School of Journalism,

> Editing for experience means, first, purposefully choosing the effects you want to create in your audience, then picking and crafting content to get those results. It applies not just to news content, but ads as well. But haven't newspapers always edited for effect? Yes they have, but the criteria have come largely from the content creators at the newspaper, not the experiences that motivate consumers to engage with the newspaper.

Lavine and Nesbitt found that by a 2-to-1 ratio young adults favored an experience-oriented front page as opposed to a traditional one. The MMC/RI was eventually successful at extending this experience-based idea to other media.

In a study of local television news, funded by the Knight Foundation, the MMC found seven relevant experiences to be in play among news-watching adults.[27] They cited local television news for creating several strong experiences for individuals: It helps me relax; It makes me smarter; I trust it; I have camaraderie with the anchor; It is a part of the community and makes me feel like a better citizen; It makes me feel good; and It is part of my routine. In contrast to this somewhat narrow list of uses, the MMC identified 22 experiences, both motivators and inhibitors, believed to drive Web site usage.[28] They are highlighted in Figure 3.3.

It is important to note that this work though done in partnership with the Online Publishers Association was not focused exclusively on news

Motivators	**Inhibitors**
It entertains and absorbs me	It tries to persuade me
It looks out for people like me	It has too much
It is a regular part of my day	Its accuracy worries me
I use it for a personal timeout	I am annoyed by the advertise- ments

It is a credible, safe place
It connects me with others
It touches me and expands my views
It makes me smarter
I am turned on by the advertisements
It is easy to use
It helps and improves me
It is worth saving and sharing
It is tailored for me
It guides me to other media
It makes me feel like I belong
It is a way to fill my time
It gives me something to talk about
It is my guilty pleasure

Figure 3.3: Motivators and inhibitors of Web site usage developed by the Media Management Center

online but also included games, entertainment, and special interest sites. While this lack of differentiation may be contested by some journalists, the approach to studying *all* media—news and otherwise—as equals suggests one of the values of a uses and gratifications framework, prizing the active audience member who can choose what to use and not use based on individual preferences, attitudes, and beliefs.

On top of this understanding that the lines among media types have been blurred, if not evaporated altogether, there is another important lesson embedded in the work of the MMC. In conjunction with Magazine Publishers of America (MPA) and the American Society of Magazine Editors (ASME), the MMC focused on the essential experiences in magazine readership.[29] The real intellectual contribution of this work was that it expanded on the idea that experiences have many underlying dimensions. This, of course, complicates the idea quite a bit. We already knew that the nature and importance of the experiences varied based on the medium.

Now because the salience of the underlying dimensions may change based on the reader or user, there is even more variability possible.

Abe Peck and Edward Malthouse, both of the Northwestern University and both involved in the original experience research by the MMC, have led recent efforts to deal with the complexity of experiences especially as we think about them across platforms as impetuses to engagement.[30] Their approach—which lent attention to several different experiences including anchor camaraderie, co-creation, and "makes me smarter"—brought modern examples to bear in an important way, ultimately serving as a guide for working journalists. What it did not do is address the relative strength of these experiences in reinventing media in the 21st century. In Peck and Malthouse's edited volume, I wrote a chapter on the identity experience. We will address the fundamentals of that experience in chapter 4, but here there is an essential point to understand. I wrote, "The media that we consume are a part of who we are and how others perceive us."[31] What I could not say there was that I believe that the identity experience is paramount to the news media's survival. Uses and gratifications with its assumption of the active audience, in part, sets up such an argument. The psychological theories that will be reviewed in chapter 4 add further support, as does evidence of the changes in American society.

The fact is that individuals have changed, and journalists must respond. Beyond what we know from all the uses and gratifications and related literature, there are a number of other relevant developments. Five will be addressed here: time, the Internet, social networking, trust, and the role of geography.

First, one of the clearest ways to understand individuals' priorities is through their use of time. Time allocation theory, used more readily in other disciplines—including marketing—than our own, gives us a basis to understand the phenomenon of individuals' perspectives. According to the theory, people are either past-oriented, present-oriented, or future-oriented. This orientation is most likely developed in childhood based on family-based patterns. For example, a child raised in a family that emphasizes its historical roots—such as what happened to their ancestors during the Holocaust—is likely to develop past orientation. If a family tends to deal with reward and punishment in the moment, present orientation is likely fostered. Present orientation is the "I touch the burner, it burns me" mentality. However, if a child is taught that there is value in delayed gratification—working hard in school will help him or her earn a big reward at the end of the year—he or she is likely to have future orientation. But, of course, time orientation can be continually modified based on societal influences. What matters to us are trends among American consumers and the potential impact on journalism. What we know is that, in general, Americans favor a future-orientated perspective. This is not necessarily intuitive; the U.S. recession that began in 2008 drew attention to the American family's failure to save for a rainy day. The future orientation here, however, is more nuanced than that. It reflects Americans' desire to want the next new thing, the expectation that the future is going to be better than the past, and that success is around the next corner.

The question remains: "What does this mean for journalism?" Consider that while the majority of Americans are future-orientated, many traditional news outlets are past-orientated. Newspapers, magazines, and television stations report what has happened. This was a reasonable thing to do when there was a clear, daylong news cycle. In the first half of the 1900s, people did not know what was going on in the world, or even down the street, until the newspaper hit their front doorstep. As has been well reported, now there is a 24-hour news cycle, initiated by cable television's news networks in the early 1980s. With Twitter and mobile updates, there should probably be a new moniker: the endless news cycle. In this environment, television news has the advantage of being able to "go live," and similar attributes from the Web—breaking news, live chats, and Tweets—establish these media's present orientation, or at least their capability to be present-orientated. Efforts to be future-orientated are limited: event listings and consumer guides, maybe this is why people favor this content in almost all reader studies; the weather forecast; and some punditry television, which attempts to predict outcomes or behavior especially of politicians.

Journalism's failure to address its public's future orientation is not its only shortcoming. Print news products are fighting against a trend away from reading altogether. The key finding of a 2007 report from the National Endowment for the Arts (NEA) was that Americans are reading less.[32] There are two ways to quantify this trend, by time and by books. First, the average time spent reading in 2006 for those 15 years old and older was 20 minutes on weekdays with a slight increase on weekends. Time spent reading on weekdays increased steadily with age: 7 minutes for those 15 to 24 years old, 9 minutes for those 25 to 34 years old, 12 minutes for those 35 to 44 years old, 17 minutes for those 45 to 54 years old, 30 minutes for those 55 to 64 years old, and 50 minutes for those 65 years old and older. Second, among almost all age groups, the percentage of adults who read a book not required for work or school fell from 1992 to 2002: down seven percentage points to 52 percent among 18- to 24-year-olds, down five percentage points to 59 percent among 25- to 34-year-olds, down seven percentage points to 59 percent among 35- to 44-year-olds, down three percentage points to 61 percent among 45- to 54-year-olds, down one percentage point to 58 percent among 55- to 64-year-olds, down one percentage point to 54 percent among 65- to 74-year-olds, and up (the only movement against the trend) two percentage points to 44 percent among those 75 years old and older.[33] As we know, newspapers and newsmagazines have not fared well in this environment.

Among journalists who are less than interested in time allocation theory, the most common explanation for people turning away from reading in general and reading print news more specifically has been the Internet. An April 2009 article on a poll by the *Atlantic* and *National Journal* of media insiders had this headline, "Media Insiders Say Internet Hurts Journalism."[34] It offered these qualitative responses from the Internet naysayers who comprised 65 percent of the respondents:

- "The Internet has some plusses: It has widened the circle of those participating in the national debate. But it has mortally wounded the financial structure of the news business so that the cost of doing challenging, independent reporting has become all but prohibitive all over the world. It has blurred the line between opinion and fact and created a dynamic in which extreme thought flourishes while balanced judgment is imperiled."
- "A year ago, I would have given a different answer. The increases in audience reach and communication with the audience are incredibly gratifying. But the cost to the business model (R.I.P. *Seattle P-I*) and the inability of the business model to monetize the Internet means that there is a disturbing net cost to newsgathering. If you're not covering your state delegation in D.C., or the state legislature back home, or the city council, bad things are going to happen, undiscovered."
- "News consumption depends on news production, and I don't see anything on the Internet that produces news—that is, detailed, responsible, empirical journalism—the way newspapers do (or did). It is typical of Americans to get more excited about consumption than about production."
- "The Internet trains readers to consume news in ever-smaller bites. This is a disaster for newspapers and magazines."

The first three of these are about the production of news and the business model, something that will be addressed in a later chapter. The last truly gets at the heart of the changes among news consumers. The Internet has been part of altering once-established patterns of behavior. How exactly that behavior has changed—and how the audience has taken control of their information gathering and news use—is the crux of chapter 5. For now, there are three changes embedded in the new media era that are also relevant to our understanding of the individuals that make up the audiences and their potential uses and gratifications. They are related to trust, social networking, and the role of geography.

First, an erosion of public trust in institutions is not a new phenomenon. Nor is attention to it. Sociologist Seymour Martin Lipset and CNN political contributor William Schneider coined the term "the confidence gap" to define a crisis in authority in the 1980s.[35] According to the team, the public's trust in business, labor, the press, and government tends to rise and fall in unison with the Watergate years being a notable exception when the press rose in esteem. The General Social Survey, conducted by the National Opinion Research Center roughly 25 times from 1972 through 2006, continues to ask people if they have "a great deal of confidence, only some confidence, or hardly any confidence" in social institutions, including the press, allowing us to examine current trends. Across the course of time, almost all institutions—except the military and the scientific community—have seen a loss in the public's trust. Let us look at the press more specifically. When measurement began in 1973, 23 percent of respondents said they had a great deal of confidence in the press. Table 3.1 details the percentage change since then.

Despite a notable uptick in 2006 in confidence in the press, the overall trend of trust in the press is downward. One supposition about the overall decline in confidence is that leaders who engage in untrustworthy behavior are to blame. The most readily used examples are in politics. Remember the examples of "journography" in chapter 1: South Carolina Governor Mark Sanford, New York Governor Eliot Spitzer, and U.S. Senator from North Carolina John Edwards. Of course, not all the troubles in politics are confined to the bedroom. Problems with money, power, and the combination of the two are all too common as well. In addition, the most recent American recession brought to the center stage of controversy some of the country's business leaders: Richard "Dick" Fuld Jr., former chairman and chief executive officer of Lehman Brothers; Earnest "Stan" O'Neal, former president, chief executive officer, and chairman of the board of Merrill Lynch; Angelo Mozilo, former chairman of the board and chief executive officer of Countrywide Financial; and George "Rick" Wagoner Jr., former chairman and chief executive officer of General Motors. It is more difficult to pinpoint blame on the leadership of our media institutions. The trouble is speckled throughout: inaccurately reported stories for the sake of speed (the "balloon boy" story of 2009 was *really* a hoax), exaggerated details and altered photos to add drama and interest (the *Time* magazine cover of O.J. Simpson's mugshot darkened to make him look more ominous), fabricated stories (Janet Cooke's coverage of an eight-year-old heroin addict named Jimmy for which the *Washington Post* eventually returned its Pulitzer Prize). The media overall bears their burden in their weakening relationship with the public, and there is no doubt that the public's use for the media has been compromised.

Second, in an environment of declining trust in institutions in general and the press specifically, there has been an upsurge in the connections among individuals. Twitter and Facebook are defining the newest paths into

Table 3.1
Percentage of those expressing a great deal of confidence in the press,
1973–2008

Year	Percentage	Percentage Point Change from Previous Year
1973	23	
1974	26	+3
1975	25	−1
1976	29	+4
1977	25	−4
1978	20	−5
1980	23	+3
1982	19	−4
1983	14	−5
1984	18	+4
1985	19	+1
1986	19	0
1987	20	+1
1988	17	−3
1989	15	−2
1990	16	+1
1991	11	−5
1993	10	−1
1994	11	+1
1996	9	−2
1998	10	+1
2000	10	0
2002	9	−1
2004	10	+1
2006	17	+7
2008	9	−8

Source: General Social Survey

the world of social networking as of this writing but the pace of innovation leads to alternative means being invented nearly every day. Through these sites and other technology—chat rooms, e-mail, blogs, and bulletin boards—users shape their social networks. Some of these technologies also allow the sharing of those social networks in public forums. What is important to understand in the context of uses and gratifications is that people use online media for a *variety* of gratifications, some similar to news consumption and some new. Moreover, the uses and gratifications model's assumption of an active audience is undeniable with this new technology. The Internet is designed for active use and prized for interactivity. The new media age is the age of the active audience.

Third, because the audience members are making media use decisions based on their needs, it is essential to examine how those needs may have shifted. In reference to local news, there is one important variable: geography. Commitment to a community—be it a neighborhood, town, or city—is likely to have an influence on the uses associated with local news. And Americans definitely have a reputation for being restless. Despite this, evidence from the Pew Research Center for the People and the Press proves that there actually has been a long-term decline in moving among the U.S. population due to its aging and more recently, the economic downturn.[36] More than two-thirds (37 percent) of people have never left their hometowns; and 57 percent have not lived outside of their home state. But likelihood of moving increases with education and income. More than three-quarters (77 percent) of college graduates have moved at least once as compared to 56 percent of those with a high school education or less. Those with a college education are also more likely to have lived in multiple states, indicating a more significant geographical gap from their birthplace. In addition, America's most affluent are the most likely to have moved, 66 percent among those earning more than $75,000. The purpose of the next chapter is to examine the phenomenon of community attachment more closely and its underlying theories.

What is clear is that the media world has changed. And today's active audience is making media choices every day. For example, in 2008 network television news combined for an average of 22.8 million viewers a night, 273,000 fewer than the previous year. The good news for the networks is that this loss actually indicated a potentially positive trend of less steep decline. From 1983 to 2008, the audience for network television news slid by about 1 million people per year. At the same time, the U.S. population has grown an average of 2.8 million people per year. In light of this, journalists must be ever mindful of the uses their readers have for their work. In addition, they must recognize the audience's perspective that the gratifications once provided by the journalist's work may be more easily, more quickly, or more adeptly served by a competitor, even a nonnews competitor. As such, journalists interested in building an audience must attend to creating meaningful gratifications.

The historical and current motivations for journalism use offer the initial indication that there has been a shift in priorities from the community to the individual. In this chapter, we explored an array of evidence including scholarly literature on uses and gratifications such as early diary approaches to understanding news consumption and more advanced studies that developed typologies of media use behavior. The underlying premise of these works is that people who find a product more useful are more likely to use it, and targeted products tend to be more useful. In fact, specialized media including narrowly cast magazines like the epicurean magazines we discussed in chapter 1 have performed relatively well by comparison to general-circulation media such as the food section in your local newspaper. This is in part because newspapers have subscribed to the community-first model, effectively ignoring individual-based needs at the core of media experiences.

CHAPTER 4

Why the Audience Does What It Does

A bird doesn't sing because it has an answer, it sings because it has a song.

—Maya Angelou

Much of the conversation about the future of news quite appropriately has focused on the role of geographic communities. Even if local television news and newspapers also include some attention to national and international affairs, local news is still fundamentally geographically oriented. *Local*, of course, is in the description. As such, the arguments being made in defense of local news are that coverage of community institutions—government, schools, courts, emergency agencies, businesses, cultural services, and civic groups—is essential to ensuring the integrity of the behavior and practices within them. In addition it is argued that an engaged, informed public is able to vote with its feet, its dollars, and its ballots at the local level to enact change. While it might be difficult in an environment infested with unethical behavior throughout the financial sector, rampant spending by government, and underperforming public schools to see the prosocial impact of news, local news advocates would rightly remind you that conditions could be much worse.

And now we are actually faced with that dark alternative. The relationship between news and community is imperiled. Picard summarized in 2005: "The economic changes and financial pressures on media have significant implications for citizens' understanding of the world, for public discourse, and for the development and maintenance of social communities."[1] The challenge outlined by Picard comes as part of what many scholars see as an undeniable change in the concept of community, which can now not only be geographic (cities, towns, and neighborhoods) but virtual (discussion boards, Web sites, and gaming networks). Virtual communities often mean the absence of face-to-face communication, which is seen as one of the pillars of geographic communities. Instead, virtual communities favor computer-mediated messaging through the Web and other emerging technologies such as mobile. In a November 16, 1988, *Wall Street Journal* article, futurist Thornton May foresaw the power of these communicative technologies as so strong that he claimed, "Geography is dead." Now executive director and dean of the IT Leadership Academy at Florida State College at Jacksonville, May predicted then that "by the year 2008, technology will have trivialized the concept of 'place.'"[2] Although perhaps not as drastically as May suggested, today people's relationships with the places they live and work are certainly changing.

In 2006 I researched the role of geography in the current news environment. I found that geographic sense of community was stronger than online sense of community, regardless of the extent of respondents' online news use—indicating that May's predication was at least somewhat overstated.[3] Still, the context provided by his prediction and my findings is more complex and worthy of a fuller understanding. Specifically, I was interested in the idea that the relationship between online news and communities might be different than the relationship between print news and communities. But perhaps it would be useful to first review what is known about print news and communities. There is actually a full literature on this dating back to the late 1970s, most of which proved something fairly intuitive. People with a high sense of community connection—oftentimes older, married homeowners—had an associated interest in local news and were therefore likely to be newspaper readers. More recent research in 2001 by Leo Jeffres, Jae-woo Lee, and Kimberly Neuendorf of Cleveland State University and David Atkin of the University of Connecticut indicated that the relationship remained valid.[4] Even when controlling for intermediating social variables, the team found newspaper readership to be positively correlated with community involvement, attachment, activities, and assessment. Community connection in these cases was entirely geographic.

But other community connections, including those that are demographic and psychographic, also lead to individuals' media choices. Local and national ethnic media are a clear example of this. Evidence from the Project for Excellence in Journalism's 2009 report of its ongoing study, the *State of the News Media*, confirms that ethnic media tend to cover the news differently than nonethnic media.[5] Depending on the nature of the audience members, that may mean more attention to happenings in their native countries, more news about the ethnic community, or particular attention to the community's perspectives or interests. It is fair to say that ethnic media prize their role as strengthening the voice of their respective communities and cohesion among their members. Unfortunately there are fewer and fewer ethnic media outlets with significantly sized audiences in America. In New York and San Francisco, the Chinese-language newspaper *Ming Pao* closed, and *Hoy New York*, a Spanish-language paper, went to an online-only production. In San Francisco, *AsianWeek*, an English-language weekly for Asian Americans, and *San Francisco Bay View*, which calls itself the "national black newspaper," eliminated their print editions. In Chicago, the *Chicago Defender*, once an influential daily newspaper with a circulation of about 250,000 at its height, shrunk to weekly distribution with a circulation of about 10,000. In addition, Linda Johnson Rice, chairman and CEO of the venerable Johnson Publishing, owner of *Ebony* and *Jet*, indicated in late 2009 that the financially troubled magazines might be up for sale.[6]

There are, however, new entrants and success stories in the ethnic media marketplace, although all typically smaller in scale and lesser in national impact than their predecessors. As an example, New America Media, founded in 1996, serves as an online aggregator of ethnic media, which it enhances with original content. There has also been substantial growth in the availability of news products for other disenfranchised groups both in print and especially online. One ripe area is the lesbian, gay, bisexual, and transgender (LGBT) community. To this, Rob Cover of the University of Adelaide in Australia established young adults' attachment to lesbian and gay print media as providing a sense of belonging in the community but also as a precursor to desiring social interaction.[7] His suggestion was that these publications were only part of the community equation. This is an important point because it drew attention to the chicken-and-egg debate that remains unsettled regarding the pattern of causation between sense of community and media use, which has never been proven. In the case of the local newspaper, does a strong sense of community cause people to read the newspaper? Or does reading the newspaper lead to a strong sense of community?

Even early research on newspaper readership and sense of community was confounded by this question. Sociologist Robert Park focused on the concept of community integration: the idea that readership leads to community connection.[8] The debate is so circular, however, that Park actually argued both sides. In the publication where he hypothesized that readership habits precede community ties, Park also offered this alternative colloquial explanation of community ties determining newspaper choice: "The farmer, it seems, still gets his news from the same market in which he buys his groceries. The more mobile city man travels farther and has a wider horizon, a different focus of attention, and, characteristically, reads a metropolitan paper."[9] Park's ability to trace community connectedness both *through* readership and *from* readership still had one important shortcoming when trying to apply it in the context of today's multimedia environment. His sense of community was purely *geographic*. Before long, there was another lens on the readership-community question. Sociologist Robert Merton expanded the concept of community connection to include interpersonal relationship and emotional ties.[10] Merton's efforts became foundational to the research of Keith Stamm of the University of Washington, who provided in 1985 what has been the definitive model connecting readership to communities.

Stamm strategically conceptualized the literature to this point as from either one of two perspectives: newspaper use led to community ties, or community ties led to newspaper use. Stamm then presented what now seems like an obvious question, but at the time it was an important intellectual step forward: "Why not a paradigm in which newspaper use both precedes and follows from community ties?"[11] Stamm represented this as cyclical relationship: Those who read their local newspapers are tied to their communities; those who are tied to their communities read their local newspapers. In this context, Stamm defined community ties as the links between individuals and elements of the community. These links, according to Stamm, exist via place, process, and structure. For example, an individual may be tied to a place through employment, to process through voting, and to structure by being a political party member. Stamm's point was that ties are definitive—seen through specific behaviors and memberships, for example. Together, these community ties and newspaper readership created a virtuous cycle. To a newspaper person, it did not really matter where or why a reader enters the cycle—whether he or she is tied to the community first or not—only that the relationship with the community is mutually beneficial.

The aim of the work I undertook in 2006 was to determine if Stamm's model was valid if newspaper use was swapped for online news use, a common behavior of media substitution among audience members today. The setting of this research was Maricopa County, Arizona, the home county of the *Arizona Republic* and its affiliated Web site, azcentral.com. This was a particularly good place to ask a print versus online question because the newspaper has excelled at online development since the launch of its Web site in 1995. In addition, via the Web it had been attentive to expanding neighborhood news—to use an old newspaper term, zoning—online. At the time of this study, azcentral.com offered 14 local area subsites in addition to a Spanish-language portal, highly differentiating the Web site from the newspaper. And while the results cannot be used to generalize about other news outlets, there were some telling findings. First, there was a correlation between sense of community and reading the newspaper. Individuals with a heightened sense of community were more likely to be regular readers of the *Arizona Republic* and vice versa.[12] Stamm was right. However, there was no relationship between sense of community and readership of azcentral.com. Stamm's model, it proved, was not universally applicable. It failed when dealing with online journalism. To be fair, Stamm's model was developed when Ronald Reagan was still president of the United States, *Back to the Future* was the year's largest-grossing film, and the first Nintendo Entertainment System was released. But what do we have to replace it? Nothing thus far. I believe that the answer is a focus on the audience via the identity-based model of journalism.

And one of the most important elements of the identity-based model of journalism is its flexibility to evolve with technology. Whether it is the Apple iPad or some innovation we cannot at this time even imagine, there is always going to be something that shakes the branches of how journalists do what they do or how audiences receive the news that they consume. We have seen the impact of technological changes already on actions that are very important to the core of journalism: how reporters gather news, how news outlets disseminate news, and how journalists interact with their readers and viewers.

The identity-based model of journalism puts forth the approach that although *the how* is a moving target, *the why* should never be. Journalists should report, write, present, and engage for the audience. The audience members are the why.

But no journalist would—or should—tolerate a model that says of the audience, "give them whatever they want." Such an approach, remember, is the worst representation of the market model of journalism. To develop an alternative—the identity-based model of journalism—we still need to know more about individuals' motivations and behaviors. The uses and gratifications model, which was addressed in the previous chapter, offered some insight. In addition, at the foundation of this research are some important theories that expand on how we understand communities and sense of community in particular. Thoughtful conceptualization of these constructs will be key to a new identity-based model of journalism. As a first step, it is necessary to define community. In the mid-1950s, sociologist George Hillery Jr. made the most substantive attempt at pinpointing a definition of community.[13] He reviewed 94 definitions of community from the literature up to that time and identified 16 underlying concepts. He found only one unifier: people. Despite this important step of pinpointing people as the essential element of a community, Hillery's definition of community remained essentially geographically bound. Remember this was the 1950s, the first time more Americans traveled by airplane than by train. Hillery's "limitation" was understandable.

In the 1980s, two psychologists, David Chavis and John "J.R." Newbrough, introduced a new perspective: "A community should be defined as any set of social relations that are bound together by a sense of community."[14] Because it is relationship-based as opposed to geographically based, this definition allowed for communities that are today part of our online culture, even though Chavis and Newbrough knew nothing of what would become the World Wide Web. What is significant about this approach is that it framed communities as bottom-up developments. It posited that the existence of small interwoven relationships created a larger community. Essentially it was the theory of the whole being greater than the sum of its parts. Popular author Steven Johnson helped us understand the "theory of emergence," as it became known, as really a theory of self-organization. And he established the geographic community as a self-organizing entity: "Cities are blessed with an opposing force that keeps the drift and tumult of history at bay: a kind of self-organizing stickiness that allows the silk weavers to stay huddled together along the same road for a thousand years, while the rest of the world reinvents itself again and again. These clusters are like magnets planted in the city's fabric, keeping like minds together, even as the forces of history try to break them apart."[15] From this bottom-up perspective, Johnson—writing in 2002, almost 15 years after Chavis and Newbrough—argued that the Internet is increasing individuals' interconnectedness.

This interconnectedness is something we intuitively know to be true. For example, the average Facebook member currently has 130 friends.[16] You may have more, many more. To contextualize this phenomenon, networking expert Albert-László Barabási of the University of Notre Dame did a modern replication of what is known as the six degrees of separation study to examine the number of relationships that on average separate one person in the United States from another.[17] The well-known version of the six-degrees study—not that of actor Kevin Bacon—was conducted by Harvard University professor Stanley Milgram in the mid-1960s, but the approach appeared in the literature back in the 1920s.[18] Milgram, who actually never used the phrase "six degrees of separation," selected two target individuals in Massachusetts. He then sent letters to a batch of people in the Midwest asking if they knew one of the two East Coast target individuals. Knowing, it is important to note, meant knowing on a first-name basis. If the recipient did not know the target individual, he or she was asked to send the letter—now a chain letter—on to a person he or she thought most likely to know or at least be a step closer to knowing the target individual. The recipient was also asked to send a preaddressed postcard back to Milgram and his team. From here, each subsequent recipient created a chain back to one of the two target individuals. With this data, Milgram determined that the median number of individuals separating a random citizen in the Midwest from one of the two target individuals was 5.5. That was 1967.

Thirty-five years later, Barabási reworked Milgram's study to examine the interconnectedness of the Web as a relevant parallel. Barabási found in 2002 that there were only 19 steps separating any one Web page from any other Web page. When you think about this in the context of the vast Internet, a distance of only 19 links is remarkable. Personal connections online made via e-mail, social networking sites, or bookmarking a favorite blog made relationships much closer than that, of course—many people and places only one click away from the user. According to Barabási, the world was *shrinking* because the number of online social links was *increasing*. The extension of this argument is that the world continues to get smaller and smaller as new technology enters the marketplace. Thomas Friedman took this tack in his analysis of globalization in his well-known book *The World Is Flat*, which was released in its third edition by Picador in 2007, but we can think about it on a more individualistic level. Twitter, for example, makes celebrities directly accessible to their audience with of-the-moment 140-character or less messages. Consider the February 2009 *Times* of London's list of top five Twittering celebrities by number of followers: (1) comedian Stephen Fry with 98,616 followers; (2) cyclist Lance Armstrong with 53,813; (3) pop singer Britney Spears with 53,290; (4) news anchor Rick Sanchez with 48,825; and (5) basketball player Shaquille O'Neal with 46,296.[19] Of course, this is a constantly moving target—both who is on the list and their number of followers—but the point is that there is access and information flow the world has never seen previously, now creating and maintaining connections among people.

Despite online connections being a modern phenomenon, the roots of the idea date back to the 1970s and scholars' attention to sense of community. To understand that area of research broadly, one must know that sense of community is conceptualized as a human emotion. It is neither a construct of place nor of relations. The construct is a specific attempt to capture the *feelings* evoked by a community, an impression created collectively by an individual's physical environment, emotional relationships, and concept of self. This complexity in the concept of sense of community was born in tandem with the articulation of the idea itself. Psychologist

Seymour Sarason, the seminal author in this area, offered this explanation of sense of community:

> [It] is a phrase which is associated in the minds of many psychologists with a kind of maudlin togetherness, a tear-soaked emotional drippiness that misguided do-gooders seek to experience. *And yet there is no psychologist who has any doubt whatsoever about when he is experiencing the presence or absence of the psychological sense of community.* . . . You know when you have it and when you don't. It is not without conflict or changes in its strength. . . . Sense of community is not a mystery to the person who experiences it. It is a mystery to those who do not experience it but hunger for it.[20]

What is interesting about Sarason's approach is that he simultaneously established that, while sense of community may be difficult to understand conceptually, everyone should want it.

The conceptual limitation set forth by Sarason has since been addressed in a more refined definition of sense of community that appeared first in an unpublished manuscript by David McMillan, a clinical psychologist in Nashville and adjunct faculty member at Vanderbilt University, and later in the research of McMillan and David Chavis, now principal associate and CEO of the research company Community Science in Gaithersburg, Maryland. McMillan and Chavis wrote in the mid-1980s: "Sense of community is a feeling that members have of belonging, a feeling that members matter to one another and to the group, and a shared faith that members' needs will be met through their commitment to be together."[21] The definition itself did not lend any utility to the sense of community construct, but McMillan and Chavis went on to pinpoint four dimensions that could be measured: (1) membership, (2) influence, (3) integration and fulfillment of needs, and (4) shared emotional connection. While measuring sense of community is not essential to a new identity-based model of journalism, understanding these four elements can provide instruction.

While the nomenclature of membership suggests a dues-paying model, like at a gym or in a professional organization, McMillan and Chavis really focused on membership as feelings of belonging. That is, individuals often know if they fit—and if *others* fit—within a group because they share common traits, make similar choices, or engage in the same rituals. Such characteristics or behaviors may be overt such as initiation to a club or traditional ethnic dress. Other examples are subtler, such as word choice or shared ambitions. The value of these characteristics or behaviors is that they define the sociological boundaries of a group or community. According to McMillan and Chavis, "The boundaries provide members with the emotional safety necessary for needs and feelings to be exposed and for intimacy to develop."[22] Within those boundaries, feelings of emotional

safety, a sense of acceptance, and a willingness to make a personal investment can develop. In addition, within those boundaries there is a role for
the other three of McMillan and Chavis's concepts: influence, integration
and fulfillments of needs, and shared emotional connection.

Influence is a concept that relies on a back-and-forth component. It extends the concept of belonging brought forth by membership to suggest
that individuals must really have a sense of ownership of the group. Since
ownership is not always something associated with communities, we can
think of this more as the ability of individuals to influence the group to
behave or react in a specific way. In addition, communities must be cohe-
sive or have the power to influence their members. Hence, there is the bi-
directional nature of influence.

The next concept, integration and fulfillment of needs, expands attention to the individual-group relationship based on the idea that being a part
of the group must be rewarding for its members. McMillan and Chavis took
this a step further to identify three primary reinforcers of individuals' engagement with groups: status, competence, and shared values. Status, generally recognized as social positioning, includes both the heightened social
perception of being a member and the impact of collective success on
increased togetherness. Competence addresses the concept of attractive-
ness, where people tend to favor group memberships that offer the most
benefit to them. Expanding on the shared values reinforcer, McMillan and
Chavis posit the following causation: "When people who share values come
together, they find that they have similar needs, priorities, and goals, thus
fostering the belief that in joining together they might be better able to
satisfy these needs and obtain the reinforcement they seek."[23] Status,
competence, and shared values collectively suggest that individuals pur-
sue communities or groups as avenues to feelings of success. The overarch-
ing assumption is that individuals feel more powerful and more capable in
communities.

The strength of community emerges again in McMillan and Chavis's
fourth and final concept: shared emotional connection. According to the
team, shared emotional connection is "the definitive element for true
community" and is defined as a link to a common history, although they
are careful to state that the history itself may not be shared, but rather a
sense of identification with shared past or similar backgrounds.[24] At the
most basic level, this form of social unity constitutes group or community
bonding around mutual histories leading to a shared present, which is also
essential to sense of community.

Taken together, these four constructs reaffirm the emotional nature of
sense of community. They parse out particular elements that are essential to individuals' feelings of attachment through membership, influence,

integration and fulfillment of needs, and shared emotional connections. Another way to understand them is to examine the subsequent development of a measurement tool. The first measurement tool related to sense of community—and the one that is relevant here—came from a research team of McMillan, Chavis, and others.[25] They recognized that sense of community was challenging to measure and therefore used an infrequently employed method called Egon Brunswik's theory of probabilistic functionalism, which relies on a set of judges' responses to variables associated with a phenomenon to establish its key characteristics. With this approach, a list of 23 predictors of sense of community was developed. They are detailed in Table 4.1.

You see among the predictors many of the traits associated in the literature with increased likelihood of newspaper readership. In fact, many researchers have since used the *Sense of Community Index*, a measurement tool that developed out of this early work, to examine the relationship between community connection and mass media use.[26]

Since the relationship between newspaper readership and community is well established, the interesting extension of this research addressed the role of the Internet and the emergence of online communities. Some have suggested that sense of community is very much alive in these virtual communities. For example, an examination of a cerebral palsy e-mail support group provided evidence that a sense of community as originally defined by McMillan and Chavis could exist online.[27] A study of eBay in 2002— seven years after its first online trade—proved that the Web site had successfully constructed a commerce community where trust was as foundational a value and practice as it was in any good, safe geographic neighborhood.[28]

Other researchers, however, have been less confident about the clear role of sense of community in these online forums. The preponderance of this work asserts the claim that digital groups—researchers on this side rarely even use the term *community* in this context—are weak because there is little or no face-to-face communication among members. E-communication, they argue, lacks the socioemotional context of physical interaction. By way of example, the Web log that eventually led to the 2009 movie *Julie & Julia* starring Meryl Streep and Amy Adams was the subject of a study conducted by Anita Blanchard of the University of North Carolina at Greensboro.[29] Blanchard examined the Julie/Julia Project, a blog written by New York City resident Julie Powell cooking her way through *Mastering the Art of French Cooking*, Child's famous first cookbook. Blogs, of course, are constructed around a central figure—the author—and therefore do not necessarily connect readers with one another. Using an adapted sense of community index, which substituted "blog"

Table 4.1
Sense of community dimensions[a] and predictors[b]

Dimensions	Predictors
Membership	Mean level of neighbor interaction
	Involvement in church group
	Involvement in business or civic group
	Involvement in PTA
	Involvement in youth groups
	Involvement in community centers
	Involvement in charity or welfare organizations
	Involvement in neighborhood organizations
Influence	Perception of block's ability to solve problems
	Influence person feels he or she has on improving block
	Involvement in political clubs or organizations
	Involvement in issue- or action-oriented groups
	Level of political efficacy
	Sense of civic duty
Integration and fulfillment of needs	Perception of block attributes
	Satisfaction with block
	Importance of what block is like
	Degree to which block meets needs and values
Shared emotional connection	Whether own or rent home
	Length of residency
	Involvement in social or card-playing groups
	Mean of close neighborly contacts
	Planned length of residency

[a]Dimensions from McMillan and Chavis, "Sense of Community."
[b]Predictors from Chavis, Hogge, McMillan, and Wandersman, "Sense of Community through Brunswik's Lens."

for "block," Blanchard measured readers' sense of community. She found only a moderate sense of community overall. More important, she made a clear distinction between two groups of users: those who actively posted to the blog and experienced a strong sense of community, and those who only read the blog and did not share these experiences. Blanchard, therefore, found interaction to be key and in the absence of interaction, an online Web site to be lacking a sense of community.

While this remains a highly contested and actively researched area, a conclusion can be drawn from what is already known regarding the identity-based model of journalism. In all of this work, still no one has established the direction of causation between media use and sense of community. They either approach with the assumption that sense of community is a result of some media use, or that sense of community is a motivator of media usage. Does this remind you of the situation Stamm was faced with in 1985? It should, and Stamm's work therefore offers an applicable framework. Just as Stamm established a cyclical relationship between community ties and newspaper use, we can think about sense of community both preceding and anteceding from media use as shown in Figure 4.1.

Again, it does not matter where people enter the cycle, only that they are in it. The trouble is that the relationship does not apply to every media outlet. If it did, newspapers would not be closing faster than the ink off the press can dry, and my research in 2006 would have found a relationship between sense of community and online news use.

What we need is a means to understand people's motivation to belong to a community or group, and the value of media to that membership. That would help us understand how journalists could craft products that fit into the virtuous "media use–sense of community" cycle. Interestingly, this guidance does not come from mass communication but from psychology—specifically, social identity theory (SIT). To summarize: SIT tells us that people have both personal identities and a biological need to maintain positive social identities. British social psychologist Henri Tajfel devel-

---

sense of community >>>>> media use >>>>> sense of community
and
media use >>>>> sense of community >>>>> media use
or, more succinctly
sense of community <<<<< >>>>> media use

Figure 4.1: Proposed relationship between sense of community and media use

oped SIT and pointed out at its outset this context: "We shall understand social identity as that part of an individual's self-concept, which derives from his knowledge of his membership of a social group (or groups) together with the emotional significance attached to that membership."[30] Tajfel explained the practical ramifications noting that, because people are driven to maintain positive and satisfying social identities, this affects their willingness to either stay a member of a group, adjust their interpretation of the group to better serve their social identities, or ultimately change groups if they can. Based on this early explanation, the power of social identity over behavior becomes clear. But the question remained: "What is the impact on mass media use?"

In fact, SIT has been used by mass communication researchers to study media use. One of the interesting directions this body of research has taken has been what might be called a merging of the uses and gratifications model, discussed in the previous chapter, and SIT. Remember, uses and gratifications has been traditionally used as a justification for individuals' media choices, the idea that individuals seek out media for the purpose of satisfying specific tangible and intangible needs. Because uses and gratifications is *only* a model, it is strengthened by a union with SIT, which is a theory. Jake Harwood of the University of Arizona explained it clearly: "[S]ocial identity gratifications are one determinant of media choices."[31] Specifically, individuals choose media that suit their social identities and avoid media that are an ill fit. The implication is that more than interpersonal interactions contribute to the construction and maintenance of one's social identity. Mass media play an important role, and researchers have since explored this concept through a variety of different social identities including ethnicity, race, and age.

Ethnic identity is the degree to which one feels connected to one's ethnic group, and the Latino identity in particular commanded the attention of researchers in the 1990s. There were some interesting results of that work. For example, media messages including images, stories, entertainment, and advertising all played a role in the construction and maintenance of ethnic identity. The same proved true in research on age identity and racial identity. One of the more interesting of these studies was run by Sotirios Bakagiannis and Mark Tarrant of Keele University in the United Kingdom. They addressed the social impact of media choice among young adults. The work was done in 2006 but is even more apt today with the buds of so many MP3 players and iPods in so many ears. According to Bakagiannis and Tarrant, "musical preference makes an important contribution to the formation and maintenance of social identity by providing individuals with a basis for social comparison and self-evaluation."[32] In their experimental study, they found adolescents judged groups who shared their musical preferences more favorably than those groups who did not. And the evidence suggests that we can extend these principles to other mediums and other groups. In fact, one of the fundamental traits of journalism—its tendency to cover conflict—puts it center stage as an actor impacting individuals' formation of identity. Vincent Price of the University of Pennsylvania explained: "In short, mass media messages reporting group conflicts of opinion may trigger social categorization, inducing people to think of themselves and others in relation to the issue as group members."[33] We see this frequently in political reporting coverage. Attention to health care in the media, for example, tends to be framed as Democrats versus Republicans as opposed to a focus on the issues at hand. News consumers watch or read this coverage and mentally fit themselves into the political group context ("I'm a Democrat so this is how I'm supposed to feel about this issue, and my Republican friend feels a different way"). This tendency for broad political categorization is why stories that run against the expected—a Democrat acts like a Republican should—are particularly interesting to media producers. The people's election of Republican Scott Brown in the special Massachusetts Senatorial race in January 2010 exemplifies this juxtaposition because the state's voters have such a liberal tradition. Democrats are supposed to vote for Democrats, not Republicans. The tension created when expected behavior is rebuffed is ripe for media coverage. Throughout narratives such as these, the media are powerful players in communicating normative behaviors, eliciting group reactions, and establishing boundaries among groups.

Although this conclusion is important in our conceptualization of the power of media in general and journalism in particular, most essential to the identity-based model of journalism is another line of SIT research: media selection. Again, there are examples of this work that addressed a variety of identities. We know from the work of Harwood, for instance, that age identity had an impact on television viewing choice.[34] He determined that the choice of shows was influenced in part by individuals choosing programs that featured characters in their age group. In addition, Thomas Ruggiero and Kenneth Yang of the University of Texas at El Paso found a positive relationship between Latino identity and Spanish-language media use.[35] People choose media in part because they suit their social identities.

In evaluating the large body of research on SIT and media use, which has been briefly reviewed here, it is clear that general media choices may be a part of social identity construction and maintenance in two ways. First, individuals may choose media that reinforce their positive social identities. But this is not a "one-media outlet fits one-identity" solution. People can have many social identities. Think about yourself as an example. You may social identity <<<<<>>>>> media use

Figure 4.2: Proposed relationship between social identity and media use

have one social identity at work, another at home, another with your friends, and so forth. Take a step further to realize that at work you probably have more than one social identity depending on the people, setting, and circumstances. A meeting with your boss to discuss your role in an upcoming project evokes a different social identity than a casual lunch with colleagues. You can, I am sure, imagine many more situations. What we do know is that these social identities may be formed via ethnicity, age, personal preferences and tastes, lifestyle factors and choices, and for an array of other reasons. We also know that media choices help define individuals' social identities. In essence we are confronted with the same issue Stamm faced in 1985. What came first, the media choice or one's social identity? So why not the same solution? Consider the reciprocal relationship posited in Figure 4.2.

It suggests that social identity is both a cause of media use and caused by media use. With the caveat that media use is not the only factor in social identity and vice versa, this is a reasonable idea. But so far, all we have from this are academic ruminations. What journalism needs is an actionable model.

I will offer first an actionable word: *relevance*. What all of the relationships reviewed in this chapter have in common is that they connect people to content that matters to them. Research conducted in 2002 by the Knight Foundation on orchestras offered a framework to think about how the research in this chapter applies to the practice of journalism.[36] Penelope McPhee, formerly the Foundation's vice president and chief program officer, explained: "The mere existence of an orchestra in a community does not contribute to its vitality. Communities need vibrant, *relevant* orchestras that give meaning to people's weary, humdrum lives."[37] The newspaper analogy is clear. The key word is *relevance*.

Communities do not rely on the existence of a news outlet, but the product or products created by news outlets are being used and valued by both the establishment and the larger audience of citizens. As an extension of this argument, McPhee went on to detail an important distinction between content and delivery in the businesses of classical music and news: "But newspaper journalists, decrying diminishing subscribers, worry that the democracy is at risk because people aren't getting the news—from them."[38] Orchestra musicians and supporters came to believe a similar thing: that the broad cultural impact of classical music was being compromised because fewer people attended the live performances. McPhee explained that newspapers and orchestras were conflating the content with the delivery method. In fact, 60 percent of adults expressed at least some interest in classical music, and one-third of them listened to classical music regularly at home and in their cars. But less than 5 percent were regular orchestra patrons.[39] Is there a similar trend among news consumers? Perhaps people are interested in news, or at least portions of the larger news agenda, but are not compelled by current news products or their modes of delivery.

This chapter brings necessary attention to the underlying theories of psychology that support the notion of prizing the individual, specifically, social identity theory and the sense of community framework. Understanding the compelling theoretically grounded reasons for human behavior related to journalism use in this new community context allows a forward-looking perspective without the prejudices of intervening technologies through which a new model that prizes the individual can be conceptualized. The next chapter will review the audience's current news consumption behavior. Its intention is to demonstrate how the audience is already engaged in a new model of journalism. Journalists just need to catch up with them.

CHAPTER 5

The Audience Already Has Control

The world is a dangerous place, not because of those who do evil, but because of those who look on and do nothing.

—Albert Einstein

The trouble for orchestras detected by the Knight Foundation, and discussed in the previous chapter, highlighted a problem felt by newspapers, newsmagazines, and news programs as well: the pressure to maintain—dare grow—an audience with the infusion of new entrants into the marketplace. For classical music, those competitors have not only been alternative delivery systems of classical music (satellite radio, home entertainment systems, and iPods) but also other forms of music (rap, rock, and rhythm and blues). News organizations have seen the same trend with threats coming from new delivery channels and, simply, new information.

This concept of new information is somewhat tricky, so let us be clear: The amount of information on the Web was in volume equal to 17 times the size of the Library of Congress print collections—and that was back in 2002. There is no doubt that the intermediating years have seen explosive growth in the amount of information available. And, of course, access to information has become easier. Web search engines like Google and Microsoft's competitor Bing, which prefers the nomenclature of *decision engine*, mean simple terms can lead to an array of information from a variety of sources. Remember the challenge from Christopher Kimball of *Cook's Illustrated* to "Google 'broccoli casserole'" highlighted in chapter 1?[1] While results will vary on any given day, on November 17, 2009, such a search produced 611,000 results. The first link was for *Cooks*.com, a Web site that aggregates people's home recipes. *Cooks*.com is careful to point out in its user agreement: "Information is provided free of charge without warranty of any kind. We are not responsible for any typographical errors or omissions."[2] This means *Cooks*.com is not liable if "sugar" is swapped for "salt" or if "one-quarter pound" is accidentally cut to "one-quarter." Worried about that recipe now? In addition to the pure amount of information—a context in which it is easy to pick on the home-grown and poorly produced content—there is now more quality public and corporate data being collected and made available via online databases. Examples include real estate records, crime data, the National Sex Offender Registry, the American FactFinder tool with the U.S. Census Bureau, and Congressional roll calls. In addition, the government and organizations have become more facile at disseminating information to the press and the public. All of this contributes to the trend of new information in the marketplace.

The concept of new delivery channels in the information environment is easier to capture than that of new information. The fact is that we use at least some of these new channels of delivery every day. To quickly review some common examples: the Internet, which includes blogs, traditional Web sites, access to podcasts, streaming music and video, news aggregators, and social networking sites; new audio technology such as satellite radio and MP3 players; mobile devices with Internet access and texting ability; and hand-held technology including Apple's iPad and e-readers like the Kindle from Amazon. Moreover, there are relevant examples that are less widely used, often due to high costs to the consumer or because the technology is still in development. From these examples, it is immediately clear how intertwined new media are with one another. For example, an individual may use the Internet in a matter of minutes to access online reviews of e-readers at a Web site like *cnet*.com, decide to get the Kindle, log on to Amazon.com to buy it, and then rely on the online retailer to purchase a newspaper's Kindle edition before she uses its 3G wireless capability to download more newspapers, magazines, books, and blogs. The interconnectedness among delivery channels has been exciting for the consumer—who can often move frictionlessly across platforms—but daunting for a traditional news organization that can "lose" audience members as they move on to alternative sources of information, potentially never to return. Consider, for example, the newspaper industry's near-abandonment of the book review section of the paper. The *New York Times* and the *San Francisco Chronicle* were the only two major newspapers to maintain stand-alone print book sections as of the end of 2009.[3] There was simply no role for these sections in the interconnectedness of delivery channels described previously. Amazon.com, the most prominent alternative, could provide review on any book at any time.

There are two interesting ways to look at the impact of new information and new delivery channels: via the news industry and via the audience members. Given the fast pace of innovation and dissemination of technology—the first IBM personal computer was introduced in 1981, less than 30 years ago—traditional news organizations have evolved quite slowly. The first online sites of newspapers appeared in the 1980s. These early sites were rudimentary, neither interactive nor particularly well designed. They were simply online presences for the newspapers. Today, while models vary, even now these sites are typically designed to complement the parent print news product, especially at small- and mid-sized news organizations. Very often these Web sites either reprint the news from the daily newspaper or aggregate it from other sources, so that little authentic original journalism is being done on newspaper Web sites. Take as an example the *East Valley Tribune* in Mesa, Arizona, and its efforts beginning in January 2009 to replace its seven-day-a-week broadsheet subscription model with a free, four-day-a-week, two-section tabloid edition.[4] According to a *Presstime* article on its plans, the *Tribune* planned 80 percent of the distribution for home delivery and 20 percent on racks. But what about the Web? People can access an online replica of the print edition on the newspaper's Web site using its e-Trib viewer.[5] That means virtually no added value vis-à-vis content. This approach is simply about access, the same as it was in 1994.

In defense of ignoring potentially added value online, news executives loudly cite troubles in the economics of media as a barrier to online innovation. In fact, the business of media has been the focus of the preponderance of conversations about the future of news in the country today. Specifically, print journalism is an expensive proposition. This cost statement refers not only to the content—reporting, writing, and layers of editing—but also to the production and distribution. And as long as online advertising lags print advertising in revenue, expending effort online feels a bit futile. More attention to this gap will be addressed later, but the important point is that these circumstances ultimately created resistance to innovation, the very innovation that the journalism industry needs to survive.

As long as journalism remains bound by the social responsibility model of journalism, "how do we pay for it?" will be the most poignant question in journalism. It is necessary to shift the discourse to the actual act of journalism—and specifically *improving journalism for the audience*. There are already some examples of the use of the Web's advantages—immediacy, interconnectivity, and interactivity—by traditional and nontraditional news organizations and nonnews organizations. These deserve attention in the context of a new identity-based model for journalism.

The *Chicago Tribune*, for example, launched *ChicagoNow*.com in the summer of 2009 in the midst of its bankruptcy. *ChicagoNow*.com breaks from traditional newspaper-produced content to engage users via social media. The site specifically encourages citizens to communicate with fellow citizens, using the tagline "It is a blog by and for locals." The blogs aggregated at *ChicagoNow*.com include *Message from Montie*, written by a Chicago lifer, vegetarian, and author of two books, with a particular interest in stories related to the African American community; *In Fashion with Barbara Glass*, a style maven with a local reporting history; and *The Barbershop* with Dennis Byrne, a freelancer and regular contributor to several political Web sites. While many contributors have experience writing—and even reporting—they are not *Tribune*-endorsed journalists. But *ChicagoNow*.com purports its purpose is not to break or even report news, but to be local and to aggregate local voices via the blogs and their comments. It presents a new value proposition for newspapers.

But the idea of newspaper bringing value to the marketplace by connecting people to one another is not exclusive to Chicago. *WashingtonPost*.com went about this in a different way when it became the largest-circulation newspaper to integrate Facebook Connect on its Web site. Its approach focused on news content and encouraging the acts of sharing and conversation. Specifically, users click on any story on *WashingtonPost*.com and are taken to a registration page. There they either enroll with a user name and password or they can utilize the Facebook Connect feature allowing them to log in using their Facebook user name and password. The advantage of Facebook Connect (for the newspaper and the user) is that users can then share content and related comments with their Facebook friends. Goli Sheikholeslami, general manager and vice president of Washington Post Digital, explained the benefits this way: "Facebook has more than 200 million active users worldwide [400 million as of April 2010], and providing a way for those people to connect to our site through Facebook promotes a more robust conversation about our content beyond the walls of our site."[6] The *Washington Post* is, of course, like other outlets not simply concerned with engagement from a standpoint of encouraging citizens' participation in democratic discourse. It is using techniques such as Facebook Connect as a viral marketing tool, whereby people spread news and their associated comments via their social networks.

Beyond the approach of connecting users to one another, there is the tactic of directly connecting users to content. Such was the focus of the *Atlanta Journal-Constitution*'s launch of *EveningEdge*.com. In January 2008, the paper introduced the Web site as a service to users trying to answer "What's for dinner?" *Eveningedge*.com is refreshed daily, relying on material from the newspaper's "Food & Drink" section. It has a complementary print publication delivered to nonsubscribers on Thursdays and also offers a daily e-mail option. With this, the *AJC* is extending its brand to nonnews, or feature, content.

Some online approaches, however, focus on production of content rather than its distribution. And in many cases the efforts of traditional news organizations to engage their audiences have taken the form of literally engaging audiences. This trend has been known under the larger umbrella of *citizen journalism*, although this term often refers to stories wholly produced by members of the community, and the phenomenon includes much more than that. For example, CNN has branded its citizen-engagement efforts under the moniker "iReport." The goal is not for these stories in and of themselves to serve as news but to enhance the network's reporting and make participants feel a part of the process. Its pitch to users:

> iReport invites you to take part in the news with CNN. Your voice, together with other iReporters, can help shape what CNN covers and how. At CNN we believe that looking at the news from different angles gives us a deeper understanding of what's going on. We also know that the world is an amazing place filled with interesting people doing fascinating things that don't always make the news. That's why iReport is full of tools built to share stories that are happening where you are and discuss the issues that are important to you. Everything you see on iReport starts with someone in the CNN audience. The stories here are not edited fact-checked or screened before they post. CNN's producers will check out some of the most compelling, important and urgent iReports and, once they're cleared for CNN, make them a part of CNN's news coverage. (Look for the red "CNN iReport" stamp to see which stories have been vetted for CNN.) Together, CNN and iReport can paint a more complete picture of the news. We'd love for you to join us. Jump on in, tell your story and see how it connects with someone on the other side of the world.[7]

Trouble is, though, not everything is vetted. That is part of CNN's approach. The network saw the implications of this in October 2008 when an anonymous user posted a report that Apple's Steve Jobs had suffered a heart attack. The report was proven false but not before the computer company's stock price dropped 10 percent in 10 minutes (it recovered to close only 3 percent lower than opening).

Among journalism practitioners and scholars there are different opinions on the issue of whether news organizations should allow unconfirmed information to be published under their brand, and if they do, the implications. Regarding the iReport-Apple story, for example, some credited iReport users who caught the Jobs's error, citing it as evidence that crowdsourcing worked. Others maintained that the cable news network risked injury to its reputation because false information was published on its Web site even if it that information was marked and supposedly distinguished as citizen-produced content.

Even with the potentially negative implication of injury to credibility, news organizations are not shying away from engaging citizens in content creation. Perhaps because they feel like they cannot ignore it. Everyone seems to be jumping into the game. In one of the more interesting examples, YouTube launched YouTube Direct, an open-source application that allows professional news organizations to broadcast YouTube clips on their Web sites. Newspapers (the *San Francisco Chronicle* and the *Washington Post*), television news programs (*ABC News*), radio stations (National Public Radio), and Web sites (*HuffingtonPost*.com and *Politico*.com) have already utilized the technology.[8] In many cases professional news organizations are simply using YouTube as a host where they post their own content and then link to it but now everyday citizens are also capturing images of news with their mobile devices or Flip cameras. Instead of just sharing them on social networking sites, those citizen producers have an opportunity to have their work professionally validated when it is rebroadcast from YouTube on a news Web site.

The balance of professional journalists and citizens heavily leaned toward the latter at the Chicago-based, nonprofit *Chi-Town Daily News* (*ChiTownDailyNews*.org), which presented a new model for news creation. Three professional editors led a small team of experienced journalists who covered education, the environment, public housing, and health. But a cadre of volunteers who were trained by the *Chi-Town Daily News* across a series of weekend short courses reported on neighborhood-based news. Interestingly, even in what might be considered a crowded media marketplace such as Chicago, the *Chi-Town Daily News* offered the only regular beat coverage of the Chicago Housing Authority and the Chicago Board of Education. Despite this success in coverage, however, it cannot be ignored that the *Chi-Town Daily News*, which was funded primarily through grant money from the Knight Foundation, found its professional-citizen hybrid financially unsustainable. In September 2009, two and a half years after the organization received initial $340,000 foundation funding, editor Geoff Dougherty laid off his professional reporters and moved to an exclusively citizen-based model. He also began efforts to find a nonprofit buyer with the intention of selling *ChiTownDailyNews*.org—its name, content, and other assets—and started a for-profit reporting venture, *Chicago Current*.com, to cover Chicago news. As of January 2010, there has been no buyer and no new news posted at *ChiTownDailyNews*.org.

There are other examples of for-profit, hyperlocal news organizations. *Patch*.com is staffed by professional editors, writers, photographers, and videographers to cover community news in California, Connecticut, Massachusetts, New Jersey, and New York. All the material is hyperlocal even though the site is owned by AOL. If a reader clicks on the Maplewood,

New Jersey, link (aka *Maplewood Patch*), news of Maplewood and relevant neighboring locales is all he or she will get, nothing far-flung. This creates a Web site with a particularly hometown feel. High school sports news, announcements of Alcoholics Anonymous meetings, calls for volunteers, classifieds, and store openings all are newsworthy at *Patch*.com.

Finally, some online efforts only tangentially deal with content but are really just tools to simplify and streamline the audience's access to news. *Everyblock*.com has received ample national attention for its combination of a hyperlocal focus, like *Patch*.com, as well as a mechanism for aggregating news from a variety of different sources including public databases. Funded by a $1.1 million grant from the Knight Foundation, *Everyblock*.com expanded from a simple Chicago-based startup to a multicity platform for geographic-based data aggregation. It utilizes online databases and search mechanisms to deliver news from sources including the local government, press releases, media coverage, reviews on *Yelp*.com, and lost-and-found postings on *Craigslist*.org. What is innovative about this is that the material is organized by address, neighborhood, or ZIP code. It is designed to answer people's questions about what is happening near where they live and work. Adrian Holovaty, formerly of the *Washington Post,* and creator of *Everyblock*.com explained: "We have a very liberal definition of what is news. We think it's something that happens in your neighborhood."[9] Holovaty and *Everyblock*.com apparently make a winning combination. He sold the Web site to *MSNBC*.com in August 2009 for an undisclosed sum.

The launch of *RealClearPolitics*.com was another example of this aggregation-based phenomenon. The Web site was founded in 2000 (remember, an election year) by John McIntyre and Tom Bevan. It is a "smart" aggregator of political news, commentary, and polling data from across the news industry. Typical links come from an array of sources: CNN; Andrew Breitbart's *Big Government* blog; and the Manchester, New Hampshire, *Union Leader.* The "smart" part of the aggregation comes from human scanning. *RealClearPolitics*.com does not rely on computer algorithms to pull together headlines like most aggregators, including those used by *Everyblock*.com. Its aggregation comes from good old-fashioned reading and decision making; it is a strong formula. In fact, the Web site garnered a following of political insiders and became attractive enough to be purchased by Forbes Media in 2007.

Other online tools are still in their infancy. For example, *Newsmixer*.us was developed as part of a project at the Medill School of Journalism for the Cedar Rapids, Iowa, *Gazette* designed to stimulate conversations around news on the paper's Web site. *Newsmixer*.us, an open-source technology, relies in part on Facebook Connect, which we have already discussed, but also brings other tools, alternatives to news Web site's standard comment box, to bear. The first of these allows users to ask a question about the story and then reporters or other users leave answers. The second tool, called "quips," takes its cue from Twitter. By invoking a 140-character limit, it forces short responses about a story from users, who select a related verb from a preselected list—thinks, wonders, agrees, disagrees, loves—and then express a brief thought. The final outlet for reader interaction is via a short (250 words or less) letter-to-the-editor feature. The *Gazette* has been bold in its attention to the role of new tools such as these in news delivery. In March 2009, the paper's former editor Steve Buttry assumed a newly coined title, information content conductor. He explained:

> It has been clear for years that newspaper companies needed to transform their organizations. We were structured for decades as newspaper factories. Though we staffed our newsrooms with skilled professionals who became experts at specific tasks such as reporting, photography, editing or graphic arts, we were focused on producing a manufactured product each day. We had strict production deadlines and the amount of content we could publish was determined by the space available, which was heavily influenced by the price of a raw material, newsprint.
>
> Reporters and photographers always gathered more information and images than their newspapers published.
>
> As newspapers started publishing content online, we had to change some of our work in the newsroom. We added new positions specializing in operations of the Web site. We started publishing breaking news online. We published new kinds of content, such as videos, blogs and slide shows. We started covering some events live as they happened and interacting live with the public. We also started niche products such as *Edge Business Magazine*, *Hoopla* and *IowaPrepSports*.com.
>
> But our organization remained structured and focused primarily on the newspaper product.
>
> We have decided that we can best meet the challenges of the future by changing our company completely. We will have an independent organization which I lead focused exclusively on developing content from our professional journalists as well as from the community. We will publish this content digitally without editing and without the limitations of products. Another organization will plan and edit products, such as *The Gazette* and *GazetteOnline*, using content from my organization as well as others.[10]

Buttry's attention to the magnitude of the problem facing traditional news organizations marks an important tipping point: He extends the conversation beyond tools and techniques to a total rethinking of the industry.

All of these efforts—connecting readers to one another and to content, citizen-based reporting on professional news Web sites, and online tools to aid in news use—exemplify the changing nature of the relationship between news and the audience. The real change is that the audience is no longer the powerless receptor of news. The audience is now calling for innovative tools, ease of access to information, and opportunities for participation. News organizations are forced to think about audience engagement, which we discussed in the previous chapter, in a way never previously contemplated. This challenge comes with opportunities and potential pitfalls. For example, the failure of newspapers and the associated closures and cutbacks that were detailed in the first and second chapters reduced the local news coverage in their respective communities. New hyperlocal sites purport to be filling the local news gap. They are, at this time, weak substitutes. This is not to say that they are not making important steps in innovation, but they generally have weak business models and have not as of yet garnered audiences of any substantial size. In addition, as a means toward innovation, some news organizations have stepped outside of their expertise of news. This has potential downsides. First, it opens news organizations up to even more competitors. Second, it has potential to compromise the brand when a nonnews brand gets in the business of disseminating unconfirmed information. But the trouble at this turn is that the audience has control and traditional news organizations really do not know how to respond.

Let us examine this further by looking at how the audience is already engaged with news. First, the numbers: According to the Newspaper Association of America's (NAA) report by Nielsen NetRatings, during the first half of 2006, there were on average 55.5 million unique visitors to newspaper Web sites per month.[11] This was about a 30-percent annual increase, up from 42.4 million across the same period in 2005. By the third quarter 2009 the number of unique visitors for an average month grew to 74 million, only 33 percent growth from 2006.[12] Despite newspaper executives' attempts to cast the growing raw number as a strong sign of their products' audience reach, the rate of growth has slowed substantially, from a steep 30-percent upward trend line in one year, from 2004 to 2005, to a much slower rate of growth of 33 percent across *three* years, from 2005 to 2009. When asked to explain the earlier high rate of growth, technology, not content, is often credited. For example, the Pew Research Center's Internet and American Life Project cited the proliferation of broadband Internet in U.S. households as key.[13] According to its research in 2006, which more broadly measured the use of Internet for news and not just online newspapers, 50 million Americans relied on the Internet for news every day. And broadband users were the most consistent users. But broadband adoption was fairly stagnant, between 55 and 60 percent of adults in the United States, in the intermediating years. It was only in mid-2009 that broadband penetration grew to 63 percent, according to the Pew Research Center.[14]

Coupled with this increase in the number of users online is the amount of time users are spending on the Web daily. The Project for Excellence in Journalism drew attention to the fact that frequency of Internet use was increasing in 2006. Moreover, it reported then that "rather than something more people were discovering, the Internet was becoming more a part of their daily life."[15] As an extension of this, consider the trend of increased time spent with newspaper Web sites. NAA detected this a few years ago. It determined then that the time Internet users spent on newspaper Web sites was rising, averaging 42 minutes a *month* during the last quarter of 2005 compared to 36 minutes a *year* earlier.[16] Then, in 2008, Internet users reported that they read online newspapers for 53 minutes per *week* (compared to 41 minutes per week in 2007), according to the Center for the Digital Future at the University of Southern California.[17]

Because of the increases in both the number of people online and time spent there, it is often assumed that readers have abandoned the newspaper and simply adapted by seeking news online. Evidence from the Pew Research Center's 2008 biennial news consumption survey suggested the circumstances are a bit muddier than that, as they often are with human behavior. The trends of news consumption by age followed some definitive behavior patterns. According to the 2008 research, both television news viewership and newspaper readership increased with age. For television, figures grew from a low of 34 percent among 18- to 24-year-olds who got news there to 74 percent among those older than 65. For newspapers, numbers were much lower but followed the same trend line, from 15 percent of 18- to 24-year-olds to 55 percent of those older than 65. Radio news listening peaked among 35- to 49-year-olds at 43 percent, forming a small hump of a trend line with low points on the ends (25 percent among 18- to 24-year-olds and 29 percent among those older than 65). The peak is among younger adults, those 25 to 34 years old when it comes to online news, but usage was a little more level among adults younger than 64: 30 percent among those 18 to 24 years old, 26 percent among those 25 to 34 years old, 34 percent among those 35 to 49 years old, and 29 percent among those 50 to 64 years old.

To think about this more simply, the Pew Research Center categorized Americans into four groups based on their news consumption patterns: integrators, net-newsers, traditionalists, and the disengaged. Despite all the bad news in the traditional news business, traditionalists actually compose the largest news-use segment. They are 46 percent of Americans. This apparent discrepancy between the size of the traditional audience and the failings in the traditional news business is explained by understanding traditionalists' tendencies in news consumption behavior. They rely heavily on television news because they seem to understand news better by seeing it. They have a strong interest in weather-related news, and weak interest in science and technology. They tend to be older, less educated, and less affluent than integrators and net-newsers. So despite Pew's nomenclature, traditionalists are not the bread-and-butters consumers of newspapers and magazines.

Integrators, in contrast to traditionalists, are well educated and affluent. They are heavy consumers of national news, especially political news. And while integrators also cite television as their primary source of news, they also credit the Internet. They also, as a group, consume the largest amount of news. Integrators, according to the Pew Research Center, are 23 percent of Americans. By comparison, net-newsers are actually the smallest group, 13 percent of Americans. The Pew Research Center describes them as affluent, well-educated, and relatively young. In addition, more than half (58 percent) are men. They rely primarily on the Web for news and are most likely to use news clips and blogs.

Finally, the disengaged comprise 14 percent of the public. According to the Pew Research Center, they have a low interest in news and an associated low level of news consumption. The real trouble among the disengaged is the prevalence of the low-interest/low-use trend among young adults. For the 10 years ending in 2008, the overall trend was toward newslessness: 19 percent of people did not consume news yesterday in 2008, as compared to 14 percent in 1998. But the most alarming change was among adults 18 to 24 years old. For them, 34 percent did not consume news yesterday in 2008; the figure was 25 percent in 1998. The challenge is to extend this behavior-based research (who read or used what, when, and for how long?) in an attempt to understand motivations. In the previous two chapters we examined the theoretical frameworks and some data, but more data would be valuable here. Unfortunately, motivation-based studies related to news are still quite limited.

One valuable insight comes from a small ethnographic study of adults between the ages of 18 and 34 who used news at least once a day conducted by the Associated Press in 2007.[18] Of course, because of the preselection criteria of using news at least once a day, this research did not address issues related to the disengaged. But it did provide some interesting findings related to changing patterns of news consumption among the participants. First, there was a relationship between e-mail and news use. The habit of logging into e-mail was often connected to scanning the headlines at a related Web site. Another primary reason for checking the news was boredom, but like the reading that was associated with e-mail, the news use was very shallow and limited to headline reading. In addition, other examples of news use among these participants were often connected to other tasks such as working and sitting in front of a computer, driving and radio listening, and watching television where entertainment shows feed into the evening news. It is not surprising then that participants were feeling "news fatigue." The researchers described it this way, "Many consumers in the study were so overwhelmed and inundated by news that they just did not know what to do."[19] Perhaps this, in part, was what prevented participants from getting the depth they actually wanted from news. They may have been too exhausted to look for and read more material. The good news was that they wanted background and detail. The bad news was that traditional news organizations were not facile enough to provide the very information and context that should be in their sweet spot.

What is interesting about the research from AP is how it factors into news organizations' proud statements of *reach* as opposed to attention to depth. A December 2008 *Presstime* article lauded audience growth across platforms for the Iowa-based Lee Enterprises, which owns more than 50 dailies as well as more specialized publications primarily throughout the upper Midwest.[20] The article detailed the seven-day reach of newspapers and their associated Web sites in Lee's 10 largest markets, illustrating overall growth from 2007 to 2008 for all four age groups (18 to 29 years old, 30 to 39 years old, 40 to 59 years old, and 60 years old and older). Although still fairly slight, the growth of seven-day reach was most pronounced among those who used print and online, and those who used only online. The largest percentage point growth for print-online users was among the youngest group, which went from 13 percent to 18 percent. That means 13 percent of the audience of 18- to 29-year-olds in Lee's 10 largest markets read its news either in print or online in 2007. In 2008, 18 percent did so. In the same time period, the percentage of print-online users among 30- to 39-year-olds went from 18 percent to 20 percent; among 40- to 59-year-olds went from 15 percent to 19 percent; and among the oldest group went from 5 percent to 8 percent. In all cases, online-only growth lagged behind print-online growth: three percentage points for the youngest group, from 6 percent from 2007 to 2008 to 9 percent; three percentage points for those 30 to 39 years old, from 7 percent to 10 percent; one percentage point for those 40 to 59 years old, from 5 percent to 6 percent; and nearly no growth for the oldest group, which stayed stagnant at 1 percent. The important point though is not the figures. Instead, what is essential is that in promoting reach, traditional news organizations have ignored the issue of *depth* via measures such as levels of attention, engagement, and interest. But depth—reporting about issues that matter and their implications and compelling audiences to care—should be at the industry's foundation.

We must contend with the question of depth in the news environment. One way to see depth, or what can also be called engagement, is in user behavior. There are actions related to accessing, sharing, commenting, and co-creating that are relevant to our understanding of audience-news interaction. For example, RSS opened the opportunity for people to take a new approach to news consumption in 1995. Instead of going to Web sites to search for new material, updates were published in a standard format via feed-reader software. It looked something like a standard e-mail page, but instead of text messages there were stories, videos, and audio clip links. Even initially, the service had its pros and cons. It was an incredible time saver for people, especially for those who used a number of online sites for news. In addition, it allowed people to isolate the news they wanted. One could request feeds from a section of a newspaper such as sports, and virtually ignore the remainder of the content. But this isolation was also RSS's primary negative feature, perhaps not felt directly by the individual but certainly relevant in the larger picture of news consumption today. People who formerly went to a Web site to search for news were exposed to other news that they were not even seeking. Perhaps a story related to their neighborhood caught their eyes for more than a moment. RSS removed what is called the serendipitous nature of news—looking for one thing and seeing something else. Writing for *American Journalism Review*, Barb Palser of Internet Broadcasting Systems made a fair comparison between RSS and Tivo (or what we now also know as DVR).[21] Both technologies put the viewer in control but come at the expense of exposure to the larger product. According to Palser, "Tools that help viewers bypass a site's homepage will certainly influence the way Web managers think about design. Now every page on a site should be treated as a homepage since it could be the first—or only—page a viewer sees. We can expect more marketing messages, advertisements and teases on internal pages." Despite these implications, RSS has continued to evolve in several key ways.

RSS has become more widely used across the news industry and blogs. It has also been branded: A small orange box with a white radio wave symbol is now the universal marker of RSS. As previously mentioned, in early 2010 the *New York Times* offered about 160 RSS feeds in 27 categories. But the rampant spread of RSS is not exclusive to big national newspapers. At the same time, the *Quad-City Times* in Davenport, Iowa, offered 34 feeds, one on the University of Iowa Hawkeyes alone. The *Herald-Tribune* in Sarasota, Florida, had 11 feeds including three that were county-based. The Riverside, California, *Press-Enterprise*, cataloged 68 feeds by geography or topic. In addition to increases in the number of RSS feeds—a trend that has also overtaken other news and nonnews Web sites as well—the need for feed-reader software that was required when the technology launched was replaced by Web-based technology such as iGoogle, myYahoo, and myAOL. Through customized homepages people could simply create and access their RSS feeds. And these pages really became the fruition of customized news products, what people have called "The Daily Me."

Along with links to easily incorporate RSS feeds into their custom homepage, people are also finding tools for sharing content with stories at most news and nonnews Web sites. These tools began simply with an "e-mail this" feature. Using it, people were able to pass stories of interest along to the inboxes of friends, family, or colleagues with brief tailored messages. This, of course, gave way to the popular phenomenon of tracking a Web site's most e-mailed stories. Research in 2007 at the University of North Carolina at Chapel Hill tracked users' behavior on Yahoo! News and compared their preferences to producers' preferences. The study's interesting conclusions for the purpose of our discussion here:

> The most viewed stories exhibited entertainment and informational features; the most e-mailed stories often featured celebrity and odd news, which may reflect a form of social networking; and the most recommended stories contained an informational element.
> The odd news category provided 21.2 percent of the most e-mailed stories, and 34 percent of the most e-mailed stories had unusual as the main news element, resulting in stories such as "Pack of angry Chihuahuas attack officer" making the rounds of cyberspace. Yet the most e-mailed category was national/political news, demonstrating a desire to share information of importance and concern with others.[22]

Capitalizing on the social nature of news led to the quick development of several other sharing Web sites. One, Facebook Connect, has already been addressed in this chapter. It has been called by Ian Schafer writing for *Advertising Age*, "arguably the biggest thing to happen to online marketing in 2008."[23] But other social networking sites such as MySpace and LinkedIn also offer a similar news-share feature. Other Web sites have grown exclusively out of content sharing. Some of the more common are *Digg*.com, *Reddit*.com, and *Topix*.com. This trend has even emerged at the local level. *WindyCitizen*.com, a free, Chicago-based Web site, allows users to share content from a variety of news sources, which often include blogs, alternative Web sites, and local entertainment magazines. They can also rate, discuss, and e-mail these stories. The more attention stories get, the more likely they are to appear on the Web site's front page, which includes a constantly updated list of the 10 most interesting stories according to

users of *WindyCitizen*.com. In effect these Web sites allow citizens to dic-
tate the news agenda through a process that researchers call co-creation or
co-production.

Co-production actually is not exclusive to an online medium. Public
access television networks have been based on this model for years. But
the Internet has led to an explosion of audience-produced material. Ashlee Humphreys of Northwestern University examined the concept of co-
production extensively in a chapter for the *Medill on Media Engagement*.[24]
According to Humphreys, who has also studied content building at the
well-known Wikipedia as a means of co-production, there are three primary motivations for individuals to contribute material: fun, an open-source
ideology, and ego enhancement. And it is reasonable to assume that the
same reasons exist for participation in news. However, even in today's
multimedia, multiplatform world, still the most common means of co-
production in news is one of the industry's oldest: commenting. Long the
foundation of radio call-in shows, commenting in an online environment
has some similarities and difference with its predecessor.

One of the most widely discussed aspects is the anonymity of commenting. This issue also existed with radio call-in shows, which typically
required callers to use only their first name—but who knows if it was really their name? Still, call-in shows seemed to have a certain formality
associated with them. Even among many of the most contentious shows,
we might call it a level of decorum. Anonymity online, however, has cul-
tivated a different culture that is typically meaner and more personal. Consider the perspective of Bob Garfield of *On the Media* (OTM):

> While it is frequently enlightening to read the incoming [comments] here
> at *OTM*, it is also sometimes frustrating, maddening and extremely discour-
> aging. In our case, the frustration mainly stems from listeners who haven't
> seemed to actually listen before fulminating and hitting Send.
>
> Other news organizations are awash in mean, hateful and occasionally
> libelous rhetoric that makes us wonder how the free exchange of those par-
> ticular ideas contributes to the alleged democratized online ideal.[25]

Despite these issues, the real value is that commenting potentially expands the conversation to everyone who has access to the Internet.

By comparison to the pervasiveness of commenting on news Web sites,
purely citizen-produced news Web sites remain rare. For a sense of the impact of those sites that do exist, we have some scope-of-the-field research
from a study conducted by researchers from Michigan State University, the
University of Missouri, and the UNC-Chapel Hill.[26] The first phase of that
research revealed that professional news organizations' Web sites were actually more likely to allow users to contribute than citizen-produced sites.

In fact, some citizen-produced sites offered no opportunities for interactions via posting comments or even e-mailing the site's producers. In addition, these citizen-produced sites often lagged behind professional news organizations' sites in terms of levels of sourcing and frequency of updates.

Regardless of the pace of innovation or growth, what is clear is that the news industry is becoming an all-inclusive tent. We used to debate—perhaps some still do—whether nonprofessional producers of news should be provided entry. To me their admission tickets have long been stamped. And now citizens who can comment on stories and connect others to stories are inside the tent too. The new questions are how do professional news producers stand out from the crowd and how do they do so in an ever-changing environment? For example, as an extension of Web-based technologies, we now have the mobile Web, which has shaken information dissemination once again. According to research released by the Nielsen Company in November 2009, the majority of mobile phones in the United States will be smartphones by the middle of 2011.[27] That means the more simple mobile technology of texting and calling will be replaced by iPhones, Blackberrys, or Android devices in the hands of about 150 million Americans. Nielsen's projections extend to predicting smartphone use: 120 million (or 80 percent of expected smartphone users) will be using the mobile Internet and 90 million (or 60 percent of expected smartphone users) will be watching mobile video. This is just one of the new frontiers.

Journalism-use behavior reveals the fact that the individual has already taken center stage. iGoogle and RSS feeds are just examples of how people can read what they want and completely avoid what they do not want. This alone recasts the traditional journalist-reader relationship in important ways. The journalist is not the sole source of information, and the reader is no longer a passive receptor. There are important implications of these changes in behavior but the most important element is that individuals' motivations matter more than they ever did previously. So what is the model of journalism to capture the engagement that already exists, capitalize on traditional organizations' reporting strength, and create a lasting foundation to evolve with new technologies? That model, which relies on the theories, behaviors, and motivations we have already explored, is what lies, figuratively and literally, just ahead.

PART THREE

A New Model
of Journalism Is Born

CHAPTER 6

A New Framework

Only barbarians are not curious about where they come from, how they came to be where they are, where they appear to be going, whether they wish to go there, and if so, why, and if not, why not.
—Isaiah Berlin

Journalists have long contended that their work merits special protection under the First Amendment. On this specific point they are not wrong: Freedom of the press *is* essential. But they have wrongly used "special protection" as shield against change, a purpose for which it was never intended. Let us flesh out this argument and its consequences. Many journalists would likely agree with the sentiment that with privilege comes responsibility—an oft-used phrase—on the basis that it is their responsibility to protect the traditional way of doing things. That way of doing things, however, has led to the starkest circulation decline in years: a drop of more than 10 percent in the six months ending September 30, 2009, according to the Audit Bureau of Circulations. The decline was just less than 5 percent in the period ending September 2008. There were bright spots, if you can even call them that. Companies such as McClatchy posted a rise in revenue from circulation of just more than 4 percent in the first nine months of 2009 primarily because of increased prices on subscriptions and single copies.[1] This was despite the fact that its flagship newspaper, the *Miami Herald*, suffered a circulation loss of 23 percent, and its *Sacramento* (California) *Bee* lost 14 percent. Clearly rising costs to the consumer is simply an unsustainable model. As is doing business the same old way, however "special" it may be.

While attending a retreat conducted by Northwestern University's nationally recognized Searle Center of Teaching Excellence, I was brought to another way of thinking about this. In a discussion about the nature of learning on the part of research-oriented faculty, a gentleman from one of the hard science disciplines commented, "You learn something when you fail." You might have heard a similar axiom as a child from your parents. But consider his point in the context of journalism today. As a scientist, he came to this with the perspective that in failure you learn that your conceptual framework does not work. The journalism parallel: Traditional journalism outlets have failed. We addressed these troubles and their history earlier, and the conceptual framework of the social responsibility model, reviewed in chapter 2, does not work anymore.

In research there are a number of ways to proceed when faced with such failure. One means is to continue to test the old framework either in new environments or among new audiences, depending on the nature of the research question, all in an attempt to pinpoint the value of that original framework. But how many holes can you put into a boat until it sinks? It may happen quickly. It may take a long time. But sinking is inevitable. Innovation does not happen this way. The second approach is to use what you learn from the initial failure to create a *new* conceptual framework, to develop new knowledge. That innovation may mark a small step forward, in that the new model retains most of the characteristics of the old model, or it may present an entirely new approach based on the invention of an idea or the application of alternative theories. Traditional journalism companies have failed to reach a sufficient level of innovation. They have generally attempted to slowly recast the old model in an attempt to gain audience, advertisers, or both. But with each experiment, it remains the same old model.

As evidence of this, consider some of the actions taken by traditional news organizations in the face of failure. The trouble at the Hearst-owned *Seattle Post-Intelligencer* forced the newspaper to cease its print edition and move to an exclusively online model, leaving the *Seattle Times* as the only print daily in the city. Upon the launch of the stand-alone digital product, executive producer Michelle Nicolosi wrote:

> We're going to break a lot of rules that newspaper Web sites stick to, and we are looking everywhere for efficiencies. We don't feel like we have to cover everything ourselves. We'll partner for some content; we won't duplicate what the wire is reporting unless we have something unique to offer; we'll continue to showcase the great content from our 150 or so reader bloggers

and we'll link offsite to content partners and competitors to create the
best mix of news on our front page.[2]

She went on to discuss the "tremendous amount of original content" that
would be produced by a news staff of 20 (compared to the original paper's
165). She also claimed the Web site would "focus on what readers are telling us they want and on what makes *SeattlePI*.com essential and unique."
In another interview she asserted the goal to be "Seattle's home page."[3]
Despite the mention of audience, this is really an attempt to do the purported work of a newspaper—to serve an entire community—with fewer
resources for original reporting.

It is a practice we have seen again and again, even among off-line media.
According to D. Brian Burghart, editor of the *Reno* (Nevada) *News &
Review*, its competitor, the Gannett-owned *Reno* (Nevada) *Gazette-Journal*,
made the following changes in 2008: increased price per issue from 50 cents
to 75 cents for most days; decreased page size, a commonly used cost-
cutting technique; retired some big-name reporters; cut the editorial section
from two pages to one Monday through Saturday; decreased arts coverage,
investigative work, the number of reporters, the availability of the newspaper, and the news hole; and increased use of user-generated content.[4]
This "harvesting strategy"—raising prices and lowering quality—could
destroy a newspaper's market position entirely, according to UNC-Chapel
Hill's Meyer. But Burghart's response to what he rightly saw as mistakes
being made on the part of the *Gazette-Journal* was only incrementally better, akin to punching several small holes in the boat until it sinks instead
of the gash struck by Gannett. Burghart wrote: "Call me old school, but I
believe newspapers must go back to doing what they did well back when
newspapers provided a high-quality product and service. Newspapers,
when done correctly, do these things better than other media: Well-
written, accurate, day-to-day local news through knowledgeable reporting; in–depth coverage and investigative reports; insightful commentary
through known and credible columnists; cartoons; and advertising that
looks good and works for the advertiser." The news product described by
Burghart is the same product audience turned away from beginning back
in the 1970s. For whatever reasons—life intervened, stories were uninter-
esting or irrelevant, or other mediums were more accessible—Americans
have rejected this dated approach.

The new challenge is not figuring out how to garner enough support
to return to the old way of doing things. It is how to find enough energy
among today's tattered and torn news organizations to try an entirely new
way. Part of that challenge is determining exactly *what audiences want from
news*. It is the "what business are you really in" question that was brought

to the forefront of executives in a 1960 *Harvard Business Review* article by Theodore Levitt. If railroad executives had realized that they were not in the railroad business but rather in the *transportation* business, Levitt argued, the railroad business would have evolved and grown with the expansion of the larger industry. Levitt updated this principle in a 2004 *Harvard Business Review* article: "Every major industry was once a growth industry. But some that are now riding a wave of growth enthusiasm are very much in the shadow of decline. Others that are thought of as seasoned growth industries have actually stopped growing. In every case, the reasons growth is threatened, slowed, or stopped is *not* because the market is saturated. It is because there has been a failure of management."[5] And I would argue that, among media management, there has been a failure of vision.

So in search of an answer, let us address Levitt's key question: "What business are news organizations really in?" Levitt's offered us a media parallel to consider first: "Hollywood defined its business incorrectly. It thought it was in the movie business when it was actually in the entertainment business. 'Movies' implied a specific, limited product. This produced fatuous contentment that from the beginning led producers to view TV as a threat. Hollywood scorned and rejected TV when it should have welcome it as an opportunity—an opportunity to expand the entertainment business."[6] By this reasoning it is easy to see how newspaper executives believed (some still do) that they were in the newspaper business—while online competitors lopped them off at the knees. The same proved true for television news executives and most recently for some magazine publishers and editors. Now the predominant current answer to "what business are news organizations really in?" is the broader news business, a response that still lacks any specificity in the definition of news. And, I argue, not quite right in the context of today's multimedia, multisource environment.

I believe journalistic organizations are in the business of creating and curating content for a specific audience. News executives, however, still believing they are in the news business, are looking to repair what is broken in the industry by searching for efficiencies in production (cost cutting) and opportunities in revenue generation. At the heart of this approach is the belief on the part of news executives that "real" journalism is an indispensable product, and if they could just convince people of it, they would come out of the current industry freefall. News proponents' interest in news literacy efforts, which include the News Literacy Project for middle- and high-school students and the growing program at Stony Brook University in New York, is indicative of this. News literacy education is a noble effort and, I believe, an important part of education of young adults. News literacy is not, however, the savior of the news business. News literacy is not going to bring people back to news. At best, it will teach people how to evaluate and value the news they are already consuming. Instead of banking on such efforts, news executives should instead be rethinking how content—and not just the content they produce—serves those people they want to reach. They should use their leverage in their communities to develop service-oriented news products that utilize information in different forms and from different sources.

It is a difficult task because it requires a complete reinvention of the industry's approach to news. In an article about the business future of AOL after its separation from Time Warner in December 2009, *BusinessWeek* claimed that AOL's CEO "Tim Armstrong[,] may have the toughest job in media—trying to teach an old digital dog the new tricks that will make it relevant to users and advertisers."[7] Language batted around in this article: *value, content, strong selling proposition, multiple layoffs and strategies, cutting costs,* and *challenge.* And the key: "AOL faces a classic business conundrum: The original enterprise (selling Web access) is dying, but the new operation (selling ads) isn't big enough to replace it."[8] This should sound familiar if one inserts "original reporting in print" and "original reporting online." And remember AOL is already well positioned as a local news competitor with *Patch*.com (discussed in chapter 5). I do not think Armstrong has the toughest job. Journalists do. They must figure out they are not in the news business anymore, and they must figure it out quickly. The business of creating and curating content requires something different of journalists than the industry currently does—understanding and responding to an audience or audiences—and there is the associated learning curve of that new skill set. But it is only with this realization that they can move forward.

The *Columbia Journalism Review* has slapped the wrist of naysayers who blame traditional news organizations for making their own bed. "Stop the glib sniping," was the foundation of a mid-2009 editorial.[9] "Rather than punish newspapers for their sins, we should work to find ways to preserve and transfer their most important attributes to a digital era, even as we push them to adapt to new financial, technological, and cultural remedies." Underpinning this book is the argument that adaptation is *not* enough to save news. News must be redefined from a community-service proposition to one that prizes individuals' uses and gratifications for the media and the medium. Based on the literature we have reviewed, I believe that the future—a new conceptual framework for studying and practicing news—can be built around the audience. Since the first signs of trouble, traditional media companies have purported to care about the audience, the consumer, or whatever language they favor. But in attempting to understand their audiences, they have been wrongly focused on studying *behavior.* They should instead concern themselves with *motivations.* We have seen scant attention to this. The Associated Press' (AP) study of young adults' news consumption reviewed in chapter 5 is one example, but Jim Kennedy, AP's director of strategic planning, admits he did the study because it would be a "fun and entertaining" presentation at the organization's annual meeting.[10]

Instead, most of the industry-based research has focused on relevant actions: purchasing, reading, scanning, discarding, sharing, and commenting. For example, within the context of audience, there has been much written recently about capturing the power of networks, especially social networking Web sites. Micah Sifry, co-founder and editor of the Personal Democracy Forum, an online site dedicated to technology and America's changing democracy, explained: "The low-cost, high-speed, always-on Internet is changing the ecology of how people consume and create political information" and anything else for that matter.[11] Specifically, "we're poised for a revolution in participation not just in consumption, thanks to the Web. People talk, share, and talk back online."[12] In fact, according to figures from the Pew Internet and American Life Project, 79 percent of American adults used the Internet in 2009, as compared to 67 percent in 2005. And, in 2009, 46 percent of those adults online used a social networking Web site, a jump from only 8 percent four years earlier.[13] A new model of journalism, however, cannot focus exclusively on connection between media entities and their audiences, or among audience members.

A new model must be about deep audience understanding and associated relevance. Bree Nordenson, writing in the *Columbia Journalism Review,* explained the current lack of audience understanding this way:

> News is part of the atmosphere now, as pervasive—and in some ways as invasive—as advertising. It finds us in airport lounges and taxicabs, on our smart phones and PDAs, through e-mail providers and Internet search engines. Much of the time, it arrives unpackaged: headlines, updates, and articles are snatched from their original sources—often as soon as they're published—are excerpted or aggregated on blogs, portals, social-networking sites, RSS readers, and customizable homepages like My MSN, My Yahoo, MyAOL, and iGoogle. These days, news comes at us in a flood on unrelated snippets. As Clay Shirky, author of *Here Comes Everybody: The Power of Organizing without Organizations,* explains: "The economic logic of the age is unbundling." But information without context is meaningless. It is incapable of informing and can make consumers feel lost.[14]

On the basis of social identity theory and the ebbing boundaries of community, we can actually aspire to reinvent the model of journalism, using what we also know about the motivations of media use and the intricacies of the behavior itself. The model—which we shall call the identity-based model of journalism—trades communities for individuals. It also attends to the issue of relevance, which is ignored in the socially responsible model of journalism. And there is reason to believe that relevance genuinely matters. Eric Schmidt, chairman and CEO of Google, expounded on this construct in his prediction for news in 2015: "The compact device in my hand delivers me the world, one news story at a time. I flip through my favorite papers and magazines, the images crisp as in print, without a maddening wait for each page to load. Even better, the device knows who I am, what I like, and what I have already read. So while I get all the news and comment, I also see stories tailored for my interests."[15]

Who I am, what I like, and what I have already read are all forms of what we might call *frictionless tailoring*. News sites adjusting to an individual's wants and needs without the person realizing anything other than "this site really seems to understand me." An approach such as this is especially important because, as we have already established, people see media as interchangeable in serving different gratifications. Practically speaking, this means if a news organization fails to deliver pertinent and easy-to-consume news, people will go to another source. The identity-based model of journalism is therefore about individuals, not communities.

Remember that there is evidence that a model based on a direct cyclical connection between media and communities, and illustrated in Figure 6.1, is unreliable in today's environment.

But based on the general tenets of social identity theory (SIT) and specifically attention to the uses and gratifications of media, we have a new means to consider this relationship, as shown in Figure 6.2. There is a bi-directional relationship between media and identity. People use media to craft their identities, and the media reinforce people's identities.

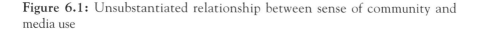

Figure 6.1: Unsubstantiated relationship between sense of community and media use

$$\boxed{\text{identity} <<<<<>>>>> \text{media}}$$

Figure 6.2: Relationship between identity and media

| identity <<<<<>>>>> community |

Figure 6.3: Relationship between identity and community

It is also reasonable within this context to conceptualize a relationship between identity and community, as shown in Figure 6.3. Again the relationship is cyclical. People belong to communities or groups because they identify with them, and their membership provides an element of identity. This is the crux of SIT.

Identity is at the foundation of relationships with media and community. As such, one of the key arguments at the heart of this book is that identity gratifications are paramount. With this, I suggest that an identity-based model of journalism, seen in Figure 6.4, is essential to the industry's future.

In the identity-based model of journalism, there are two prosocial, cyclical relationships, one between media use and identity, and the other between identity and communities. This new model updates the direct relationship between geographic communities and newspaper use detected by Stamm.

We have discussed the majority of the literature related to SIT in chapter 4, but in light of the identity-based model of journalism there is some additional context that is now important to consider. We know that two of the fundamental considerations of SIT are that individuals are constantly aiming to achieve positive social identities *and* that those social identities are obtained primarily via group membership. The latter assertion rests on the idea that the world is composed of groups. According to the psychologist Tajfel, discussed in chapter 4, "A group becomes a group in the sense of being perceived as having common characteristics or a common fate only because other groups are present in the environment."[16] Thus individuals define their social identities both by being members of particular groups and by not being members of other groups. In this context, we know that most individuals have a large number of social group memberships, and that they can be based on a variety of factors. Age, gender, re-

| media <<<<< >>>>> identity <<<<<>>>>> community |

Figure 6.4: Identity-based model of journalism

ligion, political affiliation, location of residence, and professional are just a handful of examples. Scholars have not estimated the number of social identities that an individual could maintain, but research has suggested that identities vary based on the constant changes in individuals' social environment.

Once social identities are established, the individual's focus turns toward maintaining those identities in a manner that is most satisfying. This is another place where media play a key role. We make snap judgments, for example, about someone who is carrying the *New Yorker* (an intellectual) or someone who is carrying *US Weekly* magazine (middle-brow interest in celebrities). In fact, within the aforementioned group-oriented environment, one means for individuals to secure satisfying and positive social identities is to judge their ingroups more favorably than the outgroups. That means a *New Yorker* reader is likely to feel favorably toward another *New Yorker* reader but less so about an *US Weekly* reader. "Goodness, what would they have in common?" the *New Yorker* reader might think. This is commonly referred to as ingroup bias by researchers and has been examined extensively. But what is most important with regard to the identity-based model of journalism is that individuals "experience" media in this ingroup-outgroup manner. That is, media that understand and positively reinforce an individual's identity are seen as an aspect of "ingroup-ness." And therefore members of the group are more likely to read it. But it is a double-edge sword. Media can just as easily be "outgroup-ish," a position from which it is nearly impossible to gain favor. An individual is likely to see outgroup media as ill focused because they are not focused for her, irrelevant because they are irrelevant for him, and useless because they are not useful for her. *Being for the individual* is the key.

To this point attention to *being for the individual* has become confused in discussions of media. The monikers of target or niche marketing and market or audience segmentation are not restricted to the media marketplace. Relevant in many industries, they focus on using databases to find and strategies to reach fragments of the larger market. But the challenge in the media market is that customization has been amplified many times over by both the Internet and mobile technology. Although some media such as successful magazines have found niches, it is a challenge to make customization for a group, as opposed to the individual, work. The identity-based model of journalism prizes both approaches—customizing for the individual online and creating for a community or group in print—when necessary to service the audience's needs. This is a scary proposition for journalists used to general-circulation news and something that deserves more attention. But let us first ensure that the differences between the general-circulation model and the identity-based model are clear.

One way to think about this is serving dinner in your home. Bear with me. In a general-circulation analogy, you would serve the same thing to everyone at the table. You would do this in light of your informed thoughts about both what they need to be eating for health and what they might enjoy eating as well. This may have been how meals were served when you were a child. If it was, it is likely you were admonished to finish your vegetables before you could have dessert. This actually sounds similar to the state of things at traditional news organizations today. In fact, analogies of "eating their greens" have been readily used to reflect news journalists' beliefs about news people need to know. But not everyone at the table likes everything you might serve equally, just as everyone is not interested in all the news reported for general-circulation audiences. Unlike at the polite dinner table, however, audiences are simply walking away from news sources they do not like.

To extend this analogy: A "niche-marketing meal," if we might call it that, is sensitive to the tastes of subgroups of diners. For example, among a large family meal, there might be a menu for the adults and a menu for the children. Each would be equally attentive to balance between being good for them and flavor, but the junior menu might favor simple recipes and mild spices, while the adult menu includes an alcohol-based marinade and unique ingredients. Diners might enjoy this meal a bit more than the "eat your greens" model, but basically it boils down to serving people a little of what they want and perhaps a little of what they do not. This mix of personalization and generality is still not enough to keep users committed to news media.

Serving dinner based on the identity-based model, on the other hand, is about individual tastes. This does not mean a meal of all sweets, or in news media terms, all entertainment. When you really understand someone's tastes, you can get them to eat whatever you think is best for them. It is all in how you prepare and present it. The same principles apply to news. The identity-based model of journalism is not about dumbing down the news. It is about serving individuals so well that they are getting what they want *and* what you—the journalist—think they need. In some ways then it may seem that the identity-based model of journalism is not too different from the service principle of the social responsibility model of journalism. But the important distinction is that the identity-based model of journalism focuses on serving the individual while rejecting the notion that general-circulation news has value. This is a major blasphemy for journalists, especially those working at newspapers and news stations. But let us flesh it out further.

The argument often made in defense of the social responsibility model of journalism is that journalism serves the entire citizenry. This is an important point because it is what in part distinguished journalism from other works in communication such as public relations, advertising, music, and entertainment. But it is also a fallacious argument: Journalism does not serve all citizens equally, although some media outlets do so better than others. In a study I did with the economist Dan Sullivan of the University of Minnesota, we argued that journalism outlets, focusing specifically on newspapers, should be measured using a distribution-based metric rather than a size-based metric, such as circulation, to track the equity of their impact in their community. Utilizing the Gini coefficient, which is frequently used by economists to measure income inequality as a distribution-based metric, we determined the equality in distribution of circulation of the largest 200 newspapers in 2003 and 2005.[17] We found considerable variation in how uniformly newspapers are serving their respective communities. For context, the Gini coefficient is a single number between 0 and 1 where zero represents complete equality of distribution, and 1 indicates complete inequality. The Gini coefficient based on the 2005 circulation penetration had a mean of 0.338.[18] And the average level of inequality worsened from 2003 to 2005. Consider this increase in the inequality of distribution of circulation in light of the fact that lower-penetration areas are more likely to be low income or high minority. Based on this, we argued that the purported service of journalism to a general-circulation audience was not as evenly distributed as newspapers have claimed.

In chapter 1, it was noted that some journalists are particularly adept at serving their audience. They tend to be magazine writers and editors. The business models in the magazine industry are set up to be more targeted in nature, because they are based on selling a select audience at a premium price to advertisers. Put in terms of the identity-based model of journalism, they are aggregating an audience of enough people with a similar identity, whom they can serve with a thoughtful print product. What is interesting in this context is that these select audiences need not be elite ones. There are home, hobby, and lifestyle magazines for middle-class audiences as well. Magazine editors and scholars often mention the concept of "reading up," whereby, for example, a 10-year-old girl may read *Teen Vogue*, which has a median reader age of 19. But what is essential is that *Teen Vogue* editors edit for the target identity. The 10-year-old is just gravy.

One example of stellar identity-based editing for a specific audience is *Vanity Fair*. As I wrote in *Medill on Media Engagement*:

> The fare of *Vanity Fair*: culture, politics, and fashion. But those three categories could leave the magazine within an array of pop culture products. *Vanity Fair*, instead, stands ahead of its class. This magazine is about a

sophistication, an air, a breeding, and most certainly, it's about money. An August 2009 article by regular writer James Wolcott, "What's a Culture Snob to Do?" begins:

> Pity the culture snob, as Kindles, iPods, and flash drives swallow up the visible markers of superior taste and intelligence. With the digitization of books, music, and movies, how will the highbrow distinguish him- or herself from the masses?
>
> We've all had that moment. That dial tone that hums in your head after you glance across the train aisle or spot someone perched upon a park bench or peer into the window at Starbucks and, based on the cover of the book a stranger is reading, zings the hope that he or she must be a kindred spirit, a literary soulmate, because you too dig Mary Gaitskill down to the nasty bone. Or perhaps it's *Netherland* being held like a hymnal, the acclaimed novel by Joseph O'Neill that you keep meaning to read and never will, and here it is, being read with such care by someone so cute. If only you could strike up a chat, the two of you might stroll off like French lovers thrown together by capricious fate, scampering to take cover from the christening rain. Romantic fantasy isn't the only driver of curiosity—our inner snob is always clicking away, doing little status checks.[19]

Note the embedded cultural references: There's Mary Gaitskill, who has written novels but is most well known for her essays in the likes of the *New Yorker, Harper's,* and *Esquire*. And strong, intelligent language— e. g. "capricious fate"—establish this as a magazine for those with real cultural chops.

In the same issue, well-researched articles on three tony topics appear: "the meltdown" of Sarah Palin as a vice presidential candidate;[20] the collapse of A.I.G., suggesting an ultimate villain, former executive Joseph Cassano;[21] and the many-billion-dollar loss in Harvard's endowment, which topped out in excess of $35 billion and sent jealousy whipping through the academy.[22] There are some fashion and celebrity tidbits, but even these are high tone. Consider an ode to seven movies set in the Depression, including *Paper Moon* and *The Grapes of Wrath*, but offered up in the *Vanity Fair* way, wearing Givenchy and Galliano. Oh, the irony of it all.

The real message of *Vanity Fair?* You're hipper than a *New Yorker* reader; you're smarter than a *People* reader; you're more well-rounded than a *Vogue* reader. And a *Vanity Fair* reader dies for that kind of elitism, whether or not she or he always admits it. They like for other people to know they read it (one of the behavior elements that is part of the identity experience), that they belong. Remember, part of the identity experience can be establishing who you are by who you are not.[23]

And to lend even more credence to *Vanity Fair*'s approach, there is clear evidence that this was not a one-off, one-issue effort. *Vanity Fair* ruthlessly edits for its audience with every issue. For example, the January 2010 edition touts on its cover an exclusive excerpt from the last novel from Dominick Dunne, an investigative reporter who died in 2009. Also, an inside peek at Goldman Sachs; a tale of wicked stepmothers; and a beauty shot of Meryl Streep with the quote, "I'm 60, and I'm playing the romantic lead! Bette Davis is rolling over in her grave!" *Vanity Fair* readers love it all.

Vanity Fair's success reminds us that the boundaries of relevance to the audience must be ever respected. This means two things. First, the audience will not long tolerate missing the mark regarding content, presentation, tone, or any number of other aspects. They will instead find alternate products. Remember *people view different media as interchangeable in providing gratifications*. This is a game in which only bull's-eyes win. The second point is trickier: The target is constantly shifting, even if only in incremental ways. Audience members get older; have children; have children leave home; make money; and, in the stock market of 2009, lose money. The category of parenting magazines is a good arena in which to explore this, because aging is a widely understood—and felt—concept. Audience members age out of different stages of parenting, from an infant to a toddler to a school-aged child, and so on. Clearly the content that is relevant shifts with each stage. Parenting magazines are tasked with either "aging" with their audience or earning new, read *younger*, entrants into the audience through what is called "churn," a process of losing and gaining subscribers. Either requires constant reinvention. In the case of churn, new parents in the age bracket are likely to have different perspectives, techniques, and values than those who preceded them. It is a tall task for magazines and, I would argue, for all journalism that wishes to be relevant in today's marketplace.

A keen focus on the reader is not exclusive to the magazine industry. Many Web sites have grown out of targeted interests. And while very few are original producers of news, they certainly have relevance to a discussion of the identity-based model of journalism. *RealClearPolitics*.com, which is discussed in the previous chapter, is a tool—a provider, not producer, of original content. Using human aggregating, *RealClearPolitics*.com pulls together all the headlines deemed important from across media. *New York Times* columnist David Brooks said in a testimonial for the Web site: "Some people wake up every morning with a raw egg and exercise. I wake up every morning with *RealClearPolitics*.com. It's the perfect one-stop shopping for the smartest commentary on politics and life."[24] It is the Web site of political junkies who now do not have to hop from site to site looking for what is important.

What the Web also draws attention to is the infinite ability to customize. Although *RealClearPolitics*.com does not utilize this approach, media sites could—and should—see its value. Recall, if you will, Google CEO Schmidt's call for a media outlet that knows "who I am, what I like, and what I have already read." Web sites and mobile products can use individuals' online behavior to tailor future delivery of news. We already see the actualization of this with location-based reporting. I log onto some smart Web sites, and they know I am in Chicago and deliver location-specific information. But the technology is also available to individualize my user experience based on the content I tend to favor. My interests are measured by tracking my clickthroughs and time spent reading; my preference for audio, video, or written content; and my likelihood of sharing content and via what vehicle. Then my profile can be used by an information provider to craft a unique user experience. Web sites, especially news Web sites, must use this approach to craft identity-based products that are truly audience-oriented. So although the one-size-fits-all model is dead in this media environment, outlets with an authentic audience focus can survive.

This chapter suggests a shift in thinking away from the service or social responsibility model of journalism at the historical roots of the industry to a modern approach based on individual needs. It is a fundamental change in philosophy based on a two-step flow philosophy whereby democracy and communities benefit because individuals are informed. Effectively communicating with individuals is the first, and key, step that is missing from previous discussions of how to save journalism. The identity-based model is informed by the theories and behavior presented in the previous section, agglomerating them in a unique way. The takeaway is that the best media create what we can call an identity experience. The next chapter will explore the business model for local news specifically based on this model.

CHAPTER 7

Paying for It All

When the Internet publicity began, I remember being struck by
how much the world was not the way we thought it was, that there
was infinite variation in how people viewed the world.
                                                    —Eric Schmidt

"The search for a future for serious reporting is the journalism story of our
time," wrote *Columbia Journalism Review* Executive Editor Mike Hoyt
in the September/October 2009 issue. And the majority of participants
in the national conversation about the future of news have taken this to
mean a focus on the *business model*. Potential funding possibilities have
been the subject of many symposiums, conferences, articles, blog posts, and
even 2009 Congressional hearings on the future of journalism convened
by U.S. Senator John Kerry. A portion of the Web site *Media Shift* (pbs.
org/mediashift) and its auxiliary *Idea Lab* (pbs.org/idealab), both under-
written by the Knight Foundation and well known within the industry,
have entire sections dedicated to the business of doing journalism. Shoe-
leather journalists out there reporting, writing, taking photos, designing
pages, or editing were once blind to the business side of news, citing a supposedly impermeable wall between the editorial and business functions
of a news organization. These journalists are now very aware of the dire
financial circumstances surrounding most of their work.[1] According to
figures compiled by *Mother Jones*, one in five newspaper journalists has
lost his or her job since 2001.[2]

Among all the conversations about saving journalism (and journalists), asking the audience to pay for content—along with the associated predictions about their likelihood of doing so—has been one of the issues to take its turn at center stage. This has in part come about because of the downturn in the overall economy. Before the 2009 recession, media executives predominantly believed that the equation for success online was to offer content for free and sell advertising to pay for it, although they remained perplexed by the ratio of print-to-online advertising revenue. The common figure used when describing this print-online revenue disparity was 10-to-1 in favor of print, which earned about $35 billion in revenue industry-wide in 2008. Another way to think about it is that typical news Web sites earn about 2 cents in advertising revenue per page view.[3] But what became clear as both print and online advertising declined in 2009 was that it was unlikely that revenue from the Web would ever be enough to fund traditional journalism outlets even if they went exclusively online thereby eliminating printing, production, and distribution expenses. By one estimate reported in *Mother Jones*, an online-only *New York Times* would only generate enough revenue to support about 20 percent of the newspaper's current staff.[4] This is how the "pay to play" concept came to fruition in the industry.

By the middle of 2009, real attention to charging for content began. Both Hearst and the *New York Times*—which already folded a two-year-long effort to charge for access to the work of its columnists and the paper's archives that it called TimesSelect—discussed and tested potential models.[5] Interestingly, the *New York Times'* decision to terminate TimesSelect was apparently not due to lack of income from the effort but rather lack of income *potential*. According the newspaper's own article on the shift, "The *Times* said the project had met expectations, drawing 227,000 paying subscribers—out of 787,000 overall—and generating about $10 million a year in revenue."[6] Vivian Schiller, then general manager of NYTimes.com (now president and CEO of NPR), explained: "But our projections for growth on that paid subscriber base were low, compared to the growth of online advertising."[7] The fact was that users who were brought to the newspaper's Web site via aggregators such as Google, Yahoo, and AOL were less likely to convert to the payment structure than those users who sought out the *New York Times* news directly. It is an equation that makes inherent sense: Users who seek out your brand are more likely to pay for branded content. At the time it closed TimesSelect in September 2007, the *New York Times* simply saw more opportunity in advertising revenue by giving free access to all—a decision the management of the *Times* has begun to reverse. In the summer of 2009 the newspaper sent a survey to its subscribers asking them whether they would be willing to pay $2.50

for access to *NYTimes*.com, assuming nonsubscribers would be charged $5.00. As of December 2009 access to its Web site remained free. However, in January 2010 the *New York Times* announced it would begin what it is calling a metered payment plan in January 2011, meaning that users—at least those who do not subscribe to the print edition—will have to pay a fee to access more than a few *NYTimes*.com articles a month. In addition the venerable paper was also experimenting with Times Reader 2.0, an Adobe AIR application that offers the online experience of reading the print publication, for $3.45 a week following a seven-day free trial.

In a similar fashion at the 2010 Consumer Electronics Show in Las Vegas, Hearst introduced a newspaper- and magazine-friendly e-reading device designed to receive content from a variety of publishers. The device developed by Skiff and paired with service from Sprint differs from the more well-known Kindle because it focuses on periodicals as opposed to books. In addition, it calls itself "publisher friendly" because it hosts advertising and shares the majority of the revenue. In contrast, Amazon.com keeps as much as 70 percent of the subscription price of Kindle subscription sales. The Skiff also capitalizes on another strength: strategic alliances. The Skiff and its associated services brings together once-rivals including Hearst, Time, and Condé Nast, all hoping to find means to extract revenue from digital media.

But the pay-for-content model, even when it offers the added benefit to the audience of convenient delivery, has significant challenges. The foremost of which is converting people who have been free users into paying ones. *New York Times* reporters Richard Pérez-Peña and Tim Arango offered interesting parallels of pay for "free" content. For example, "Coca-Cola took tap water, filtered it and called it Dasani, and makes millions of dollars a year. People who used to ask why anyone would pay for television now subscribe to cable and TiVo. Airlines charge for luggage, meals, even pillows. And some music fans who have downloaded pirated songs are also patrons of iTunes."[8] To be fair, these may not be perfect analogies. With downloading music, for example, the comparison is between an illegal and legal act. And cable and TiVo are offering additional services above and beyond traditional broadcast television, whether it be access to more channels or automated recording. The airline and bottled water parallels are more appropriate. They are about charging for something people used to get for free. As Pérez-Peña and Arango pointed out, "these success stories offered the consumer something extra, even if it was just convenience."[9] Priya Raghubir of the Stern School of Business at New York University offered this explanation: "With bottled water, it's a kind of snobbery and the perception of healthiness that they have marketed. With newspapers and magazines there have to be features you can't get anywhere else, and maybe part of what you would pay for is the privilege of helping the business survive, but that is a more difficult sell."[10]

The concept of *privilege*—of being part of an elite group of individuals who support journalism—has brought another funding model to the forefront: the nonprofit approach. As previously referenced, in 2009 U.S. Senator Benjamin Cardin of Maryland introduced legislation that would allow newspapers to become nonprofits under section 501(c)(3) of the tax code. The advantage of this legislation, which as of this writing is still before Congress, is that it makes contributions to these converted entities tax deductible. It does not, however, address the reality of the actual conversion from for-profit to nonprofit, which is complicated at many newspapers by their overhanging debt and other liabilities. Which is why much of nonprofit-based journalism work has come from start-ups.

MinnPost.com, a local online reporting outlet, is a prominent example of this new approach. Launched in 2007 under the leadership of Joel Kramer, former editor and then publisher of the Minneapolis *Star Tribune*, it used personal funds and money raised from local donors. With several hundred thousand unique visitors each month, *MinnPost*.com's strength is in its tight focus: "Our mission is to provide high-quality journalism for news-intense people who care about Minnesota. We intend to focus sharply on that mission, and not get distracted by trying to be all things or serve all people."[11] But with a reported budget of about $1 million annually, *MinnPost*.com must continue to attract funding from foundation grants and reader support. Similar circumstances exist at a variety of more established nonprofit journalism outlets: the Center for Public Integrity (PublicIntegrity.org), founded by former *60 Minutes* producer Charles Lewis in 1989 in Washington, D.C.; *Voice of San Diego* (*VoiceofSanDiego.org*), an online newspaper that launched in 2005; and the long-standing *Christian Science Monitor* (*CSMonitor*.com), which ended its daily print production in 2009, favoring a Web-based product complemented by a weekly print magazine.

Even some traditional journalism outlets without nonprofit status have tried to move into the donations arena. In December 2009 the *Miami Herald* began an experiment, which it has since abandoned, that asked its readers for financial contributions via an online donation site. Its plea:

> Thank you for helping to make *MiamiHerald*.com South Florida's most-read news destination on the Web. *MiamiHerald*.com features all the coverage of the *Miami Herald*'s award-winning print edition, plus breaking news and multimedia extras including video, audio, slideshows and searchable databases. If you value the *Miami Herald*'s local news reporting and investigations, but prefer the convenience of the Internet, please consider a voluntary payment for the Web news that matters to you.[12]

The point is that regardless of the source of funding—donations, advertising, or subscriptions—the issue at hand in journalism today is how to be an attractive investment and many news organizations are running business ideas though trial and error.

For example, there are a number of news organizations that have tried to offer the "features you can't get anywhere else" suggested by Raghubir, who sees this differentiation as key to financial success. In mobile delivery, we have already discussed Hearst's attempt to provide added value with Skiff, which in essence is high-quality paperless publishing attempting to preserve the design values of newspapers and magazines, a benefit missing from Amazon.com's Kindle or the Nook from Barnes & Noble. Skiff is not the only technological development in this area. The research and development team at the family-owned Bonnier Group, publisher of an array of media including *Popular Science* and *Parenting* magazines, has been working on a similar device that it is calling Mag+. In Internet-based news, the aforementioned *Miami Herald*, owned by McClatchy, has offered an array of added-value services: an interactive calendar of events; Twitter feeds associated with local news, political news, world news, lifestyle stories, sports content, and entertainment features; and a downloadable widget for a Chumby, an always-on device that relies on Internet-based widgets to deliver constantly updated content, including news, weather, social networking updates, and podcasts, based on the user's preference. And in print, the *Economist* broke new ground in August 2009 when it launched a single-copy subscription service in the United Kingdom, allowing readers to order one issue of the magazine for home delivery the next day. The antithesis of the year-long subscription model used by the industry, the program, Economist Direct, is available via online or text ordering and costs users the standard newsstand price.

There have also been print-online hybrid experiments. One, a European-based idea launched in November 2009, has been called the "customized newspaper." Developed by two German entrepreneurs, Hendrik Tiedemann and Wanja Oberhof, the newspaper allows users to register on its Web site, *niiu*.de; access content from a variety of national and international sources including 17 newspapers and hundreds of online sites; and then select the type of material they would like to read, which is organized into a printed paper and delivered the next morning. Users' preferences can be edited at any time if they feel, for example, they are getting too much sports or not enough business. The paper has a differentiated cost for students ($1.80) and nonstudents ($2.70), which seems high by comparison to American newspapers but is on par with European pricing. The interesting point is that *niiu*.de still sees value in print. "It's an individualized paper which has a wide appeal because people, especially students who grew up with the Web, want to get their news from different sources," explained Oberhof. "Many people prefer to read a newspaper; they like the feel of paper."[13]

Maggwire.com is another alternative attempting to capitalize on taking traditionally print-based media online in a customizable way. Launched in late 2009 in beta form, *Maggwire*.com aggregates articles that are available online from more than 600 magazines including *Time*, *Golf*, *Business-Week*, *Wired*, and *Entertainment Weekly*. As of this writing, access is free, but the founders Jian Chai, Steve DeWald, and Ryan Klenovich intend to convert to a paid service in 2010: Users would pay a monthly fee of $1.99 to subscribe to a specific content area and be provided with articles from across a variety of magazines. Readers would also be able to add magazines for about $1 a month or articles for between 15 and 50 cents. *Maggwire*.com plans to remit 75 percent of the revenue back to the magazines.

The reality is that an overall journalism environment plagued by failure is ripe for experimentation. And there are some efforts outside the scope of mainstream that also merit mention. A service called Help a Reporter Out (HARO.com) uses up to three e-mails a day to connect journalists with sources looking for publicity. As of April 2010, founder Peter Shankman claimed about 30,000 reporters had used HARO, and Shankman had more than 57,000 followers on Twitter where he posts requests, media-related updates, and personal tidbits. Shankman makes money, about $1 million a year, by charging for advertising at the top of each e-mail distribution. Such an approach, one could argue, degrades the traditional social responsibility approach to doing journalism by putting journalists in touch with people who want to talk and not necessarily those with the most important perspective. But it is important to note that some major news organizations including Dow Jones, Meredith, and ABC have used HARO and further that there is a business model for an approach that connects reporters with sources.

Other business-oriented suggestions have been focused on shifting content. Mort Zuckerman, owner of the New York *Daily News*, has charmingly offered a solution to journalism's financial woes: Bingo. "Just make bingo legal on our Web sites. . . . The newspapers in England are supported almost exclusively by the profitability of running bingo games on their Web sites. It attracts an enormous audience. . . . Let every newspaper do that, and they'll all make enough money on their Web site[s] to really help them stay viable. It's a simple solution."[14] There have been even more outrageous solutions. In April 2009 blogger Jonathan Mann created a video, *Saving Newspapers: The Musical!*[15] His idea: "If you wanna compete with the Internet you gotta start thinking like them. It's been tested. It's been proven. Boobs alone will get the traffic movin'. So repeat after me, 'Boobs on the front page.'"

In addition to these decidedly alternative approaches, there are also examples of pure pay-for-content models online. The *Wall Street Journal* gets the most attention, but even its story is more complicated than at first glance. A print subscription is $2.29 a week, an online subscription is $1.99 a week, and bundled they are $2.69 a week. But there are other access options as well. The newspaper began introducing iPhone and Blackberry applications in 2008, and until 2009 they were free. Now only a small amount of content is available there without a subscription. Even with this change, the *Wall Street Journal* has not successfully walled off all content entirely. *Salon*.com's Farhad Manjoo wrote in 2008 about using Google to access full-length *Wall Street Journal* articles for free.[16] And it is completely legal. Even with its free holes, however, the *Wall Street Journal*'s model is admirable. It continues to attract paid subscriptions from enough readers to support its business model. In fact, Alan Murray, deputy managing editor and executive online editor of the *Wall Street Journal*, explained at a February 2010 conference at The Paley Center for Media in New York that the money the *Journal* makes off its digital operations is double the expense of its entire newsroom. But how replicable is its model? Media insiders would tell you that the *Journal* has an unmatchable advantage in that its subscriptions are often tax deducible for business purposes. However, it should not go without mention that it also has a niche audience that it serves with a carefully crafted and targeted news product.

Without these advantages, most newspapers have not been able to produce this robust of a revenue stream from the Web and other digital outlets. Earl Wilkinson, executive director of the International Newsmedia Marketing Association (INMA), described those who do not believe in journalism's financial potential as "newspaper-phobes who hate virtually everything our industry does, believe we are going to die, and therefore advocate that all of our worthless content be free and open to consumers."[17] Among those who do find value in the product (and it need not be newspapers but journalism in general, however delivered), there are five different perspectives on revenue generation.

First, there is the option to require payment to access *any* content online. This payment could take the form of micropayments, paying a little at a time for small bits of content or services, or subscriptions. But the principle is the same—no content is free. Understanding the means to set that price either via micropayments or subscriptions still merits attention.

Micropayment is a constantly and rapidly moving target. In fact the structures that currently exist are based on a variety of different values and approaches. One of them, BeneVote, developed a voting widget for use by media Web sites. Its innovation is that it costs the user nothing. Instead, the online publisher installs the company's widget, and doing so adds a voting box ("I like it" or "I don't like it") at the bottom of each story. Readers click on one option and see a pop-up box—"Your votes help sponsor this site. Thanks!"—followed by a Google AdSense text advertisement. BeneVote is still in beta version and is owned by Silicon Valley-based Twixa, which shares its revenue with publishers based on an as-yet undisclosed basis. Other micropayment models rely on user-generated revenue. For example, Kachingle.com, also in beta version, offers a model in which users contribute $5 monthly. Contributions are distributed proportionally to the Kachingle.com-linked Web sites users use and appreciate most, allowing users to maximize a small donation across many sites. Kachingle.com also works with participating sites to acknowledge user contributions by name.

It cannot go ignored, however, that micropayment structures have not been universally well received. Most remain almost entirely unknown. Although micropayment models vary, three that received fulsome attention in the industry—Payattention.com, Contenture.com, and Inamoon.com—are already out of business. The Contenture.com site delivered the news of the December 2009 closure: "Thank you to everyone who believed in our service by installing it on their site or signing up for a paid account. Unfortunately, we were unable to get any big publishers to use the service, which was going to be the key to our success. Without any large publishers, the economics just don't work." Although it had the potential to extract revenue by aggregating users, it did not solidify a consumer base for news organizations. Because depending on the nature of the journalistic content, the crowds may come and go, micropayment ultimately incentivizes the worst kind of audience-based journalism that simply responds to the whim of the consumer and does not necessarily attend to the important news in a community.

In contrast, the subscription approach solidifies the relationship between the news outlets and the consumer. The consumer has already made the initial decision that the content is valuable to him or her. Moreover, because the subscription transaction is likely to be online, it is easier for the company to secure renewals—as opposed to the challenges of getting consumers to mail in payments historically experienced by newspapers and magazines. The major trouble, however, is that there is little evidence that enough users will convert to a subscription model to support the journalism being done by traditional news outlets.

As such, a second idea being considered is to force payment only on certain content. There are varying philosophies on exactly what content should be behind the pay wall (archives, the most popular content, or interactive features like the crossword puzzle), and even that varies by news outlet. But the core idea is that the majority of content is free and supported by advertising. This has become known as the *freemium* model— "free" plus "premium." The challenge is to determine what to give away and what to protect behind the pay wall. For example, Bloomberg, which purchased *BusinessWeek* in late 2009 from McGraw-Hill, plans to make the magazine's content free online while also creating "virtual content areas" that will offer depth in yet-undefined subjects for a fee expected to be about $100 a year.

The third approach is a derivative of the advertising-only model that most news organizations are relying on now. Called an affiliate model, it relies on a Web site's content, brand, and associated relationships with users to drive traffic to affiliated sites where purchases for tangible products are made and profits from those purchases are shared. You may have seen this approach if you read any lifestyle-oriented Web logs that recommend products. One is *IlluminatedMind*.net. It is run by Jonathan Mead, who is now earning enough revenue (about $2,000 to $3,000 a month) from his blogging to have quit his full-time job. Mead recommends products and earns revenue when his users click on the link and make a purchase. He offers this insight on his success:

1. You have to have your reader's trust. If they don't trust you, they will not buy what you recommend.
2. You have to target the products to your readers. Speak to their interests, personality and emotions.
3. You need to be able to write decent copy and communicate in a compelling way why they should buy what you're recommending.[18]

It is a bit quirky and likely not a viable option for many traditional news organizations. It might, however, be considered by consumer-based media such as magazines and specialty publications.

The fourth potential revenue model has nothing to do with the purchase of actual goods but virtual ones. If you are a Facebook user, you have likely seen an example of this with Facebook Gifts, which was launched in 2007. Users can send virtual gifts (cakes, stuffed animals, or flowers) to their friends in private or public, so that they appear on the recipient's profile.[19] Gifts are $1 each and come with the opportunity to customize a message, much like a conventional gift card. The margins, of course, are quite high because there are only an initial production and setup costs.

However, this approach relies on users of a Web site having relationships with one another such as we see with Facebook. Therefore it is likely only applicable to certain news media Web sites.

We might call the fifth and final approach the *in-betweenie* model because it is closely related to both the first (all pay) and second (freemium) approaches. Web sites give away the content but limit its redistribution and encourage payment from at least some consumers by using persuasive messaging and online contribution mechanisms. The passing-on-of-news—and worse, its regurgitation—by other Web sites have drawn much attention from reporters as well as news editors and producers. Ian Shapira of the *Washington Post* wrote an interesting piece on this dilemma in August 2009:

> A few weeks ago, I scored what passes these days for one of journalism's biggest coups, satisfying a holy writ for newspaper impact in the Internet age. *Gawker*, the snarky New York culture and media Web site, had just blogged about my story in that day's *Washington Post*.
>
> I confess to feeling a bit triumphant. My article was ripe fodder for the blogosphere's thrash-and-bash attitude: a profile of a Washington-based "business coach," Anne Loehr, who charges her early-Gen-X/Boomer clients anywhere from $500 to $2,500 to explain how the millennial generation (mostly people in their 20s and late teens) behaves in the workplace. *Gawker's* story featured several quotations from the coach and a client, and neatly distilled Loehr's biography—information entirely plucked from my piece. I was flattered.
>
> But when I told my editor, he wrote back: They stole your story. Where's your outrage, man?
>
> The more I toggled between my editor's e-mail and the eight-paragraph *Gawker* item, the angrier I got, and the more disenchanted I became with the journalism business. I enjoy reading *Gawker* and the growing number of news sites like it—the *Huffington Post*, the *Daily Beast* and others—but lately they're making me even more nervous about my precarious career as a newspaper reporter who enjoys, at least for the time being, a salary, a 401(k) and health insurance.[20]

Gawker.com had a link to Shapira's original article at the top of the page but no reference to the *Washington Post* until the very end of the post, which was almost entirely lifted. But on the upside, *Gawker*.com was the second most popular "push" to Shapira's article at *WashingtonPost*.com (a feature on *Slate*.com, which is owned by the *Washington Post*, was first). Shapira's conclusion: "I still want a fluid blogosphere, but one where aggregators—newspapers included—are more transparent about whom they're heavily excerpting. They should mention the original source immediately. And if bloggers want to excerpt at length, a fee would be the nice, ethical gesture."[21]

For reasons such as these cited by Shapira in reference to *Gawker*.com, Google has borne the brunt of the angst from traditional journalists. Rupert Murdoch announced in November 2009 that he intended to remove his company's news content from Google in order to install a pay-model for his organizations' stories. In response, Google introduced an easy solution that would allow any publisher to immediately remove its content from Google's search. As of the end of 2009, none had, not even Murdoch's News Corporation. Google is still receiving enough attention that it was the subject of a *Columbia Journalism Review* article, "What's a Fair Share in the Age of Google?"[22] Peter Osnos explained: "Google has become a kind of metaphor for the link economy and the Internet's immense power to organize content. Yet as a global leader among Web-based enterprises, it has also become a subject of debate and controversy, even though its sense of itself is still as benign as the playful tenor of its Manhattan offices, where the fittings include scooters for zipping around the halls and a lavish free cafeteria."[23] But what is important is another issue related to the Google controversy, what Osnos called "fair conduct." Here is his example:

On Saturday afternoon, February 7, 2009, *SI*.com, the Web site of *Sports Illustrated*, broke a huge story: Alex Rodriguez, the mega-rich Yankees star, had taken performance-enhancing drugs while playing for the Texas Rangers. *Sports Illustrated* released the story on its Web site rather than in the magazine, according to the editors involved, in an effort to enhance *SI*.com's standing as a destination for fans increasingly conditioned to getting sports news online. Within hours the story was everywhere, but if you went through Google to find it, what you likely got instead were the pickups that appeared elsewhere, summaries or even rewrites, with attribution. Most galling was that the *Huffington Post*'s use of an Associated Press version of *SI*'s report was initially tops on Google, which meant that it, and not *SI*.com, tended to be the place readers clicking through to get the gist of the breaking scandal would land.

Traffic on *SI*.com did go up on that Saturday and for days thereafter, but not nearly as much as the editors had projected. As long as the value of advertising on the Web is measured by the number of visitors a site receives, driving those numbers is critical, and therein lies the dilemma. Why did the *Huffington Post* come up ahead of *SI*.com? Because, even Google insiders concede, *Huffington* is effective at implementing search optimization techniques, which means that its manipulation of keywords, search terms, and the dynamics of Web protocol gives it an advantage over others scrambling to be the place readers are sent by search engines. What angered the people at *Sports Illustrated* and Time Inc. is that Google, acting as traffic conductor, seemed unmoved by their grievance over what had happened to their ownership of the story. An *SI* editor quoted to me Time Inc.'s editor-in-chief, John Huey, noting crisply that, "talking to Google is like trying to talk to a television."[24]

The rules of the road for distributing traffic on the Internet need to include recognition, in simple terms, of who got the story. The algorithm needs human help; otherwise, valuable traffic goes to sites that didn't pay to create the content.

The fact is that Google believes its approach of aggregating links with only a sentence or two of the article's content is both fair use and ultimately to the benefit of all content producers. But the original content producer is continually at risk. Deeper attention to fair use and its implications are worthy of further study, but the subject is outside the scope of both this book and certainly this chapter—in which we are attempting to resurrect the foundering business of journalism using the identity-based model.

For now most news organizations remain "in bed" with the Google model, and the fear of users refusing to pay or agreeing to pay only a very small amount for news has kept most news organizations from moving to wall off their content. An exception is the *Newport Daily News* in Rhode Island, which began in 2009 charging $345 a year for unlimited access to its Web site. This represented a firm—and high—pay wall, more than 130 percent of an annual subscription to the newspaper. Publisher Albert K. Sherman Jr. explained it this way: "We want to drive people to the print version of the paper."[25] Sherman's point is that print is where the revenue is, a theme we have previously discussed. But his paper is one of the first to actively resist readers' move to the Web with an exorbitant pricing strategy. And there is reason to believe that others will follow in a similar manner. In November 2009 the American Press Institute presented the initial findings of an ongoing online survey of news executives and their intentions to take their products online.[26] Of those responding, 80 percent of newspapers published most or all of their content online, and 90 percent said they offered free access. But nearly 60 percent were considering charging users for access to content currently available for free, and 25 percent intended to do so within the subsequent six months.

The trouble, of course, is that the Web offers so many competitors that if journalism Web sites flip the "pay-for-access" switch, they may simply push more consumers away from traditional news sites. Boston Consulting Group (BCG) offered some insight. Based on an October 2009 survey of 5,000 people worldwide, it reported that 48 percent of American respondents who were regular Internet users would pay to read news online or on their mobile devices. But the price they were willing to pay was only about $3 a month. BCG's senior partner John Rose offered this explanation: "Consumer willingness and intent to pay is related to the availability of a rich amount of free content. There is more, better, richer free in the United States than anywhere else."[27] But Rose pointed out that even though the level of payment is relatively low, "The good news is that, contrary to conventional wisdom, consumers are willing to pay for meaningful content."[28] As discussed in the preceding chapter, a clear route to producing meaningful and relevant content is understanding the identity of the audience and then creating and curating for them.

What most journalism entities have is not simply a pay problem but an engagement problem. Even worse, the media industry does not possess a universal understanding of what engagement is, although they institutively do know it matters. I recently wrote about this with two Northwestern University colleagues, Edward Malthouse and Bobby Calder.[29] We argued that the journalism industry's failure to recognize engagement as an essential metric in the modern multimedia environment has left it vulnerable to advertisers imposing a definition upon them. Consider that the Association of National Advertisers uses this definition: "Engagement is turning on a prospect (current or potential user) to a brand idea enhanced by the surrounding context."[30] By this definition, journalists' work is relegated to surrounding context. This perception is part of what has pushed journalism entities into powerless positions in the marketplace today. Malthouse, Calder, and I asserted that engagement should be defined as *the collective experiences that readers or viewers have with media*. Malthouse and Calder had done extensive work prior to this on how experiences aggregate to create engagement.[31] Their approach was based on the uses and gratifications approach reviewed previously but took an important step in isolating some media-based experiences.

As an initial step, Malthouse and Calder conducted almost 400 indepth, hour-long interviews with consumers about the function of media in their lives. Analysis of the transcripts led to the development of Likertscale items for inclusion on subsequent surveys. Malthouse and Calder were ultimately able to identify 22 online experiences, 44 newspaper experiences, 39 magazine experiences, and 12 television news experiences. That means, for example, watching television news may not produce the same set of experiences as reading print news. This, of course, confirms what we know from uses and gratifications. Table 7.1 illustrates a sampling of the specific statements made by the audience related to media use, in this case local television, and categorizes them, as Malthouse and Calder did, into easily understood experiences.

Table 7.1
A sample of experiences and specific use statements related to the audience and local television news

Experience	Item
Trustworthy	They do a good job covering things. They don't miss things.
	It is unbiased in its reporting.
	It does not sensationalize things.
	I trust it to tell the truth.
Civic	Watching the news makes a difference in my life.
	Watching the news makes me feel like a better citizen.
	Our society would be much weaker without television news.
	It makes me more a part of my community.
Positive emotional	Some stories on the news touch me deep down.
	The stories in the news affect me emotionally.
	When watching the news, I want to learn how stories end.
	I find myself wondering how things could have turned out differently.
Routine	I tend to watch television news at the same time or times each day.
	It helps me to get my day started in the morning.
	It's part of my daily routine.
	I use television news to get my news for the day.
Relaxing	I like to kick back and wind down with it.
	It's a treat for me.
	I watch it as much for the entertainment value as for the information value.
Anchor camaraderie	I enjoy watching the people doing the news talk with each other.
	I feel like I get to know the anchors on the news programs I watch.
	The anchors and reporters on the programs I watch are qualified professionals.
Hype	The local news that I watch covers accidents and crimes way too much.
	I wish they would talk less and show me more.

(continued)

Table 7.1
(*continued*)

Experience	Item
	Too much of what they do is done mainly to try to get more people to watch.
	The same stories on the news are repeated day after day.
All the same	The different news programs I watch are all very similar in the way they do the news.
	The different news programs all have the same stories.
Selective surfing	When watching the television news I try to see what stories are coming up so I can catch the ones I want to see and avoid the ones I don't.
	I always wonder what the other news programs are covering when I am watching the news.
	I pick and choose what I pay attention to on the news.
	I often turn on the news to see if there is anything going on.
Background	I like to have the television news on in the background while I am doing other things.
	When I watch the news I prefer to sit and focus on it. (negative loading)
	While I am watching, usually the activity going on in the room around me is on my mind.

Source: Peer et al., *Local TV News Experience.*

Some of the experiences are positive, termed *motivators*. Some are negative or *inhibitors*.

There are numerous nuances when it comes to understanding engagement because it is such an umbrella concept and various definitions of engagement exist. For example, a report prepared by Wetpaint and Altimeter on the world's 100 most valuable brands provided a number of ways to think about engagement purely in terms of social media.[32] The research team determined that among these top 100 brands, the more channels of social media communication they were involved with, the more likely their audience was to be engaged. But this came with some important and instructional caveats, especially as we consider business models for media companies. According to Wetpaint/Altimeter, businesses fall into one of four areas or quadrants. Picture them this way: Imagine a simple graph with a 45-degree line from the bottom left-hand corner to the upper right. This line represents the relationship between the number of channels an organization employs and level of engagement of its audience or customers. Since this is a trend line, there are actually businesses that in reality fall above or below the line. Wetpaint/Altimeter categorizes the businesses above the line into two groups and those below the line into two groups. Those with a multitude of channels and high engagement are *mavens* (Dell, eBay, and Starbucks). *Butterflies* (American Express, Nintendo, and Cisco) use a similar number of channels as *mavens* but have a below-average level of engagement. Among those with fewer channels of communication, there are those who are relatively successful in attracting engagement. They are called *selectives* (Visa, GAP, and H&M) by Wetpaint/Altimeter, while those companies that earn little engagement are *wallflowers* (BP, McDonald's, and Johnson & Johnson).

The goal for any media company is to be a maven—and therefore highly adept at using multiple channels of social media communication well. This is reinforced by the fact that Wetpaint/Altimeter was able to prove that mavens were mostly likely to have revenue growth, gross margin growth, and net margin growth from early 2008 to 2009. With this, Wetpaint/Altimeter cited Starbucks as the most successful and offered some insights on the coffee company's multichannel approach: Starbucks "realized that each channel is different and required developing different facets of the relationship with their audience."[33] Some examples: Using Facebook to encourage users to interact with one another. Relying on Twitter to provide immediate customer service and any breaking news. Creating new sites to encourage unique interaction with the brand. Starbucks has MyStarbucksIdea.com where customers submit, comment, and vote on their favorite ideas about a whole array of things including a loyalty program, recycling, coupons, sugar-free options, and WiFi access. The customers, not Starbucks, decide what is posted and discussed here. At this turn, most traditional media companies have failed to duplicate Starbucks's attention to depth across social media channels and thereby are unable to capitalize on engagement in the same way the coffee purveyor has. And engagement is the end game.

Let us examine why engagement is key. A *BusinessWeek* article on engagement, ideal audiences, and television provided some guidance.[34] It described the important distinction between the traditional metrics of Nielsen ratings, "which measure if the TV is switched on but not whether people are sleeping, snacking in the kitchen, or surfing the Web," and recall studies of programs and advertising.[35] An example:

> Like many companies, Ford has slashed its TV advertising budget. Marketing chief [James] Farley is keen to make every ad dollar resonate with potential buyers and has been striking more deals tied to a program's engagement ratings. On the face of it, Ford had little reason to advertise with the Discovery Channel's *Dirty Jobs* series, starring Mike Rowe. The show delivers puny Nielsen ratings. But when engagement metrics were applied to the program, the viewers most deeply absorbed in the show turned out to be truck-buying men aged 18 to 49, a ripe demographic for Ford. That prompted Ford to advertise heavily and hire Rowe to appear in Web video demonstrating the durability of the F-Series pickup.[36]

Television executives have been hesitant to embrace engagement metrics, citing "the need for more testing and fine tuning." But it is likely that this resistance is due at least in part to the fact that providing—and proving—engagement is a new challenge for them in an environment already marked by new competitors, new technologies, and new delivery channels.

As complicated as the concept of engagement and its measurement are, part of the purpose of this book is to assert that the media/identity experience—the way media use reinforces who we are and helps us understand who other people are—is at the very core of creating engagement. Therefore identity is key to developing workable business models of journalism. The reality is that much of the industry's efforts to emphasize the audience have come from the approach of either demarcating the audience to fit a preexisting product or developing new services for a large general-circulation audience. Instead, the industry needs platform-agnostic information delivery that responds to the audience members' stated needs and, better yet, the needs they did not even know they had. Who knew they "needed" an iPod before Apple invented it? There is no doubt there will continue to be innovations across platforms from non-media companies like Apple. Google, for example, is working on technology called Google Fast Flip (fastflip.googlelabs.com) to make reading article online easier and faster. And we have already seen Apple's iPad and HTC's Incredible smartphone. But journalism outlets must stop simply *responding* to technological changes. Journalists must understand their audiences well enough to serve them no matter where and no matter with what. Based on this argument, there remains a unique selling proposition for local news. Journalists and news executives should know their market better than any aggregator or national outlet ever will. By virtue of both their reporting and marketing, they know the groups in their communities, or what we can also refer to as the relevant identities. Local news organizations must harness this advantage. But the real change is that they cannot do it from a general-circulation, social responsibility model of journalism perspective.

Consider an example of this flawed general-circulation approach. In 2007 the *Gainesville* (Florida) *Sun*, a New York Times Company–owned newspaper in Florida, began offering an edition targeted for University of Florida students for free on weekdays when school was in session. But students were significantly more likely to read the student newspaper, the *Independent Florida Alligator*, than the *Gainesville Sun*'s campus-centric edition, according to a study by Steve Collins of the University of Central Florida and Cory Armstrong of the University of Florida.[37] Collins and Armstrong determined that more students read the *Alligator* at least four days a week than read the campus-based *Sun* even once a week. Although the research did not include a formal content analysis of the differences between the two papers, it suggested that the heavy features and entertainment content of the *Sun* was a turnoff for students. Also, students were more likely to look at the opinion pieces and the advertising in the *Alligator* than in the *Sun*. I believe that the *Sun* simply did not know the audience as well as the student newspaper did. Nor did it know what was truly relevant (local bar and restaurant advertising, for example, as opposed to national ads). The *Alligator*, being a newspaper embedded in its community, understood intricacies of content for the University of Florida students. An extension of this point is that the *Alligator* staff would unlikely be able to duplicate their success on another campus in Florida or throughout the nation, where the student identity is different. Their success is at the University of Florida for students with a high sense of identity related to the university.

Serving an audience requires true understanding of who they are and what their informational needs are. At the local level this means news organizations should select a handful of groups in their community that they can serve well. Part of this argument, of course, is the belief that they cannot serve everyone—and so out goes the social responsibility model of journalism. This idea is supported by evidence that specialized media such as subject-specific magazines have outperformed general media such as newspapers since at least the 1960s. Relevance matters. Further, in serving five to six groups well, news organizations have the opportunity to explore alternative business models for each of these groups. While these groups could—and should—vary by community, let us explore a couple of examples that might have near-universal relevance.

Among almost all local news organizations, one group to be considered an important audience are local public affairs junkies. Picard and Meyer have been proponents of focusing on this audience.[38] And while the nature of this audience will vary from community to community, we have a general sense of who they might be. These are the people who listen to NPR, subscribe to the *New Yorker* or the *Economist*, and discuss local government at cocktail parties. Based on their identity of wanting to be "in the know"—as well as wanting to tell others what they need to know—about governmental affairs and public policy, public affairs junkies are likely to be willing to pay a premium price for a product that lacks the fluff of a general-circulation product and is targeted at them and their high-brow interests. Among this likely older audience, a weekly print product with extensive analysis may have appeal, as might a free service that provides tailored electronic updates about public meetings or important votes on a daily basis.

In contrast, another group at least some news organizations should consider is the young business class, those white-collar workers who are handcuffed to their smartphones. By the very nature of their mobile tether, a news entity has an opportunity to understand this audience: busy, business-oriented commuters. This audience is less likely to pay for content in the traditional sense because they were raised in a "content should be free" generation. They do, however, exhibit a willingness to pay for mobile applications. In a study of the downloading and use of both paid and free iPod applications, Pinch Media determined that among its sample more than half of iPhone and iPod Touch devices had installed and used a paid application.[39] This suggests news organizations may find opportunities to serve a member of this group via an application that, for example, delivers real-time traffic for her commute home, or delivers the "water cooler headlines"—stories in the news that people will be talking about—every morning along with the weather report (will she need her umbrella?). She represents a "news you can use" hungry audience.

Beyond these suggestions, there are other opportunities. For communities with an influx of newcomers, a news organization might consider figuring out who they are and why they came and then craft products to serve them in their transition. Such products could be cross-platform and include a service-based real estate Web site with a depth of information about schools, services, and commuting; a four-color evergreen print magazine featuring local businesses and extensive coupons; or a social networking site driven by newcomers interacting with one another and relevant original content. Some other potential audiences: local sports enthusiasts, even high school sports enthusiasts; a cultural or religious group; a socioeconomic group; those affiliated with a certain industry or interest; those with children in public elementary schools; those who are committed environmentalists; and those who drive Suburbans. Not all of these will be relevant examples for every community, but every community has a selection of groups that news organizations can and should serve. In fact, the key is that local news organizations are in a unique position to be aware of, and therefore serve, the identities that are present in their communities.

But there remains a potential problem with these examples, according to the authors of *The Curse of the Mogul*: "Local just ain't sexy."[40] However, as Jonathan Knee, Bruce Greenwald, and Ava Seave explained, "Even in the purely geographic rather than psychographic or demographic context, the notion that the Internet eliminates borders is fundamentally misguided."[41] To this point local has been seen as not "sexy" because it has been fundamentally lacking in any application to people's lives. But "sexy" is being served with news that matters, not distracts. Relevant news must be the foundation of an identity-based product. Some of the news will be local, some will not. Some will be produced by the delivering organization, some will not. It will all be determined by the audience. To do this news organizations must study their communities closely, with a particular focus on isolating the groups they can serve and serve well. These studies should utilize quantitative and qualitative techniques, rely on primary and secondary research, and be conduced across departments including News and Marketing. The root of this audience research could be the organization's collective intuition about who its audiences are (remember, local news entities should know better than anyone), but ultimately it should rely on evidence-based research. Then using this new knowledge, journalism outlets should develop products—likely more than just a few for each group. Those products should satisfy the audience's needs with regard to editorial content and tone, graphic design, delivery vehicles, timeliness, interactivity, and related services, because in doing so news organizations will fill a gap in the marketplace. Even after this research-based design process, ruthlessly maintaining an audience-based focus is more than half of the success equation in the identity-based model of journalism. Every story, every angle, and every service must maintain an identity-based connection with the audience even as the audience evolves. The key point is that there is no one-size-fits-all model for news or the business of news anymore. Journalism organizations must be more facile and more responsive to audience needs.

Attention to workable business models has subsumed most of the conversation about saving journalism but almost the entirety of this chatter has been focused on how to monetize online readership to pay for investment in the journalistic process exemplified by daily newspapers. The fact is that investment in journalism has traditionally been markedly higher for newspapers than that for other news industries. That is, while there is little evidence that the transmission medium—print, online, or otherwise—degrades the innate value associated with the best news journalism, there is ample evidence that companies cannot make enough money from online news to support expensive journalism practices. The trouble is newspapers and news Web sites alike are trying to make money from the old way of doing things. The identity-based model proposed in this book opens new connections to users that lay the foundation for new streams of revenue with the power to save journalism.

CHAPTER 8

Journalism Is Spelled with an "I"

Action is the real measure of intelligence.

—Napoleon Hill

The social responsibility model of journalism is outdated. It did not survive the evolution of the relationships between individuals and geography nor between individuals and media. Audiences and advertisers are abandoning it. It is unsustainable and unrecoverable. Those operating news organizations on the basis of the social responsibility model are generally failing. And those who are concerned with saving it by focusing on alterations to the business model are acting in error. But the blame for this attachment to the social responsibility model is widespread. The fact is that most journalism schools still believe that the social responsibility model of journalism is the lynchpin of a career in journalism. They teach that it has current value. Most journalism students use the language of the social responsibility model—democracy, informed citizenry, public good—to explain their professional interests. Their approach is bolstered by the fact that the industry generally shares this perspective.

In 2007 the then American Society of Newspaper Editors' President David Zeeck said in a speech to the organization's members:

I believe journalism is important. I don't think free people or free societies can exist without a free press. I believe that's what journalism is for. For that reason, my newspaper will fight for open government and the First Amendment. I also believe that if we produce journalism worthy of that First

Amendment, and if we hold to our principles, if we cover our communities with affection but tell the truth, we can survive this crisis as we've survived so many others.[1]

Of course, since 2007 the crisis has only worsened. As a more current example, the Project for Excellence in Journalism suggested in 2009 that the real cause of the rot in journalism has been in the business model: "The problem facing American journalism is not fundamentally an audience problem or a credibility problem. It is a revenue problem—the decoupling, as we have described it before, of advertising from news."[2] However, I beg to differ. The problem facing American journalism *is* the audience. This is not to say that there is an "audience problem." Such language suggests that the audience is misbehaving. The audience is not wrong. They are never wrong. If an audience member does not value the work of a journalist or a journalist's organization, it is not because he or she is not smart, engaged, or a good citizen. It means the journalism missed the mark. The problem facing American journalism is that it fails to engage its audience.

This idea that the problem is the journalists and not others is, in and of itself, a completely different framework for the industry. Journalists rightly believe that they have power as agenda setters in their communities, telling people not what to think but what they should think about. This is the premise of agenda-setting theory. To state it more bluntly, many journalists believe that they tell people who are not as smart as they are, their readers, what is the important news of the day. It is an elitist perspective that is allowed—perhaps even encouraged—by the social responsibility model of journalism. But there is not space for such an on-high position in the identity-based model of journalism. Journalists must listen, really listen, to the audience, reflect on what they hear, and respond.

The idea of responding to the audience has to this point been a bitter pill for journalists to swallow. Some have simply refused, regarding it as "pandering." Most have heard it as a marketing ploy more than anything else. Some scholars have even suggested that, by responding to the audience, the industry has traded in the social responsibility model of journalism for the entertainment model of journalism. It may not be far from the truth. The evidence is there: the explosion of salacious news in late 2009 from the small town of Windermere, Florida, following Tiger Woods's car accident outside his home and the subsequent uncovering of more than 12 mistresses; the constant coverage of reality-television stars Kate and Jon Gosselin during their breakup and divorce with more attention to the controversy—the status of their TLC show, the financial riffs, and the alleged affairs—than their eight children's well-being; and the voting drama of *American Idol,* which began its ninth season in 2010, as Ellen DeGeneres replaced Paula Abdul as a judge. But I see the industry's turn to entertainment news as an attempt to retain and gain audience as a sign that the current gap between journalists and their audience is akin to a gaping ravine. Right now journalism organizations serving general-circulation audiences are using entertainment content to appeal to what they see as their communities' lowest common denominator—the infrequent or nonreader. But this approach only underlies the journalist-audience schism.

The current disconnect between journalists and their audience can even be comical. On December 3, 2009, the *Washington Post* ran a correction for an article on the hip-hop band Public Enemy's efforts to address the issue of homelessness that ran in the newspaper 10 days earlier: "A Nov. 26 article in the District edition of Local Living incorrectly said a Public Enemy song declared 9/11 a joke. The song refers to 911, the emergency phone number."[3] In fact, the song, "911 Is a Joke," was released in 1990, more than 10 years before September 11, 2001. It criticized emergency response teams for taking too long to respond to emergency calls from black communities. The error and its correction drew viral attention from sites such as *HuffingtonPost*.com ("*Washington Post* Forced to Correct Report That Public Enemy Called 9/11 a Joke"), Scott Rosenberg's *wordyard*.com ("Public Enemy and the *Washington Post:* The Correction as Folk Art and the Viral Meme"), and *Columbia Journalism Review* ("Don't Need to Wait, Get the Record Straight: *WaPo*'s Public Enemy Correction Brings the Noise on Twitter"). Much of the commentary on the mistake focused on the timing of the correction, which was slow, and the internal editing process, which was broken when a copy editor changed 911 to 9/11 without confirming the change with the story's reporter, an editorial aide for the *Washington Post.* People are correct to point out that the situation was handled poorly by the *Post.* Rosenberg explained:

> It's worth recording what this incident reveals about the disconnect between newsroom traditions and contemporary reality. . . . The *Post* followed the circle-the-wagons playbook more appropriate to a Watergate-level power struggle than a little pop-culture gaffe. It waited a week to post the correction, and it was the notice's opacity and stiff tone, as much as the original error, that exposed the paper to ridicule.[4]

Rosenberg's assessment of the *Post*'s old-school practices being unsuited to the new-school ways is accurate. But this story also presents another journalist-audience disconnect. The average age of the American newspaper reader is 55 years old and getting older. Do you think the typical 55-year-old cares about Public Enemy? Do you think he would even know who Public Enemy is? Or have any interest in hip-hop altogether? I would argue it is unlikely enough to reconsider even including such a story in a supposedly "general-circulation" newspaper that is really only read by the community's established members. The work Sullivan and I did using the Gini coefficient has already discredited the concept of general circulation meaning equal service for everyone. As such, this entertainment coverage in traditional newspapers is both out of place and a bad investment on the part of journalism organizations.

The idea that general-circulation products really do not circulate equally also refutes one of the criticisms of the identity-based model of journalism as I have proposed it. Some believe that if news organizations are charged with selecting only a small handful of audiences to serve well, the poorest, most marginal communities will be left off the list. It is at first blush a fair concern, but there is some important context and a potentially powerful response. First, Sullivan and I already established that currently newspapers do not serve geographic groups in their communities equitably. We also know from qualitative, industry-based evidence that all circulation is not equally prized. Some circulation—like some viewership—is more valuable than others. This is why newspapers with wealthy zip codes in their circulation zones often create specialized publications from their marketing departments to host high-end advertisers. Reaching the rich is more expensive—but also therefore more valuable for newspapers—than reaching the masses. For this reason, some newspapers have even shifted their general-circulation distribution. It is a long-time trend. In the mid-1990s, Merritt, the editor of the *Wichita Eagle*, was forced to cut circulation outside of metropolitan Wichita. About 10,000 county readers were cut from home delivery. In 2007 the *Atlanta Journal-Constitution* made a conscious decision to shrink its circulation area and stop increasing discounts for home delivery. A *New York Times* article called changes like these intentional: "Driven by marketing and delivery costs and pressure from advertisers, many papers have decided certain readers are not worth the expense involved in finding, serving and keeping them."[5] The fear that the identity-based model of journalism will neglect the news needs of the disenfranchised members of the community has already been realized under the social responsibility model of journalism.

But unlike the unbridgeable gap between journalists and the disenfranchised left by the social responsibility model of journalism, the identity-based model of journalism offers an opportunity to serve this audience in a meaningful way. Consider this criticism first: By attempting to serve entire communities via the social responsibility model of journalism, newspapers and television stations rarely address the concerns or reflect the circumstances of community members living below the poverty line or otherwise on the fringes of society. A browse through "Today's Front Pages" on the Newseum's Web site, which archives more than 700 newspapers from 67 countries, reveals how American newspapers are missing this audience. Here is a sampling of front-page headlines from December 19, 2009:

> At the *Birmingham News* in Alabama: "Feds Seize New South Federal," "City Police Put 'Boots on the Ground,'" "State Jobless Rates Decline," "Moore's Legal Battle for UA Continues," and "McWane Inc. Pleads Guilty to Polluting."
>
> At the *Oakland Tribune* in California: "Job Loss Becomes a Regional Story," "A Cleaner Fleet: Shipping Firm Set to Cut Emissions at Oakland Port," "Commitment in Copenhagen," "A Fiery Debate: Home, Hearth vs. Hack, Cough," and "Rate of Autism Rinsing in U.S., CDC Reports."
>
> At the *Richmond Times-Dispatch* in Virginia: "December Nor'easter Dumping Snow on Va.," "Firm Aims to Keep Ukrop's Service," and "Kaine Seeks 1% Rise in State Income Tax."
>
> At the *Blade* in Toledo, Ohio: "Bell Selects 4 Directors, Drops 1 over Unpaid Loans," "Climate Accord Falls Short of Goals," "Man Held in Kidnap of Local Pair's Son," "1,400 IT Workers at Auto Supplier Must Reapply for Their Positions," and "Karl Rove to Be Speaker at County GOP Dinner."
>
> At the *Columbia Daily Tribune* in Missouri: "Another Landmark for Battle," "Hinkson Still Listed 'Impaired,'" "Obama Brokers Climate Deal," and "One in 110 U.S. Children Have Autism, CDC Estimates."

Banking, autism, income taxes, the environment, and politics—all outside the confines of what is truly relevant for an audience struggling with maintaining day-to-day employment and taking care of their families. In general, newspapers have long been criticized for failing to serve their communities' members who are most in need with meaningful content. The reality is that under the social responsibility model truly serving the poor is an almost insurmountable challenge. Advertisers, who are the ones really paying for general-circulation news, are not interested in reaching those people who are not engaged in regular commerce. The identity-based model of journalism, however, allows a news organization to include this disenfranchised audience as one of the groups that it serves. The form of the product developed for this audience might be a weekly print newsletter focused on relevant neighborhood news especially as it relates to public services including schools and emergency personnel support; actionable information such as notices regarding public meetings; and attention to local-level leaders, not just governmental figures but also religious, community, and nonprofit leaders. It might be home delivered for free or deposited in free racks in the appropriate parts of town. Reasonably, it

may be the one branch of service that a news organization would run via
a nonprofit model, reviewed in the previous chapter. Grant funding and
personal donations, not advertising, could support this targeted service.
This is journalism in the service of an audience, and it is founded on the
identity-based model of journalism.

Because the audience is key in the identity-based model of journalism,
it shifts the power in the journalist-reader relationship. However, the
power of journalistic institutions has already been diminishing. Brand
names of many newspapers, television networks and stations, and magazines do not carry the weight of influence they once did. "People relate to
individuals more than they do to organizations," explained David Cohn,
an open-source journalism advocate and founder of *Spot.us*. "The byline
has always been there. More and more, people are going to trust specific
reporters rather than branded news outlets."[6] As such, *Spot.us* offers what
it calls community-funded reporting. In its model, freelance journalists
craft a pitch and attempt to garner financial support for the reporting and
writing using *Spot.us*, which has been called a virtual tin cup. The contributions are tax deductible, and if a news organization—the *New York
Times* has participated—buys the story, the donations are reimbursed. Otherwise, the content is made available through a Creative Commons license.
Journalists, whether affiliated with a brand name organization or not, can
exploit this new advantage of individual brand, where the journalist is the
capital. Relationships matter more than ever. The identity-based model
of journalism addresses this.

Another advantage of the identity-based model of journalism is its
flexibility. Because the identity-based model of journalism prizes the
audience—as opposed to the institution, the medium, the technology, or
the practitioners—it can evolve as the audience changes. This allows for
any circumstantial changes including those related to the demographic
and psychographic characteristics of the audience, which are inevitable.
One of the social responsibility model of journalism's failures is its lack
of nimbleness. The identity-based model of journalism attempts to overcome this shortcoming. It ebbs and flows with the audience.

Beyond this practical application, the identity-based model of journalism
has implications for how and why scholars study journalism as well. For
example, the nuances of distribution and the metrics of circulation were
fundamental to the social responsibility model of journalism. The social
responsibility model of journalism was all about reach. As such, studies
often focused on the relationship between circulation size and a number
of factors including content type, production practices, and presentation
style. The identity-based model of journalism, on the other hand, is about
impact. This means academics should shift their research to recognize this

new framework. The plethora of scholarship, some of it quite good, in the media effects arena has already recognized the importance of impact. One example from Sriram Kalyanaraman of the UNC-Chapel Hill and Shyam Sundar of Pennsylvania State University focused on an area pertinent to the identity-based model of journalism: the role of customization online. They conceptualized several potential influences of customization on users' attitudes toward a Web site. There were perceived relevance, perceived interactivity, perceived involvement, perceived community, and perceived novelty. Kalyanaraman and Sundar determined that participants were able to discriminate among different levels of customization, and that personalized content led to their positive assessment of the site.

As Kalyanaraman and Sundar's work points out, personalization of Web sites has the ability to influence users. Web sites and other media are in unique positions to provide valuable services. David Abrahamson of Northwestern University discussed the future of the magazine form and cited "magazines' unique ability to *mediate between individual interests and shared interests.*"[7] He continued:

> As the national culture continues the fractionization begun in the mid-twentieth century, the move to more niche-oriented, targeted, special-interest media will continue. But within that phenomenon, the power of magazines to define and then *create the idea of community* will become more crucial. This inextricable link between magazines and specific communities of interest will prove paramount in magazines' success. In sum, I suspect that the magazine form will have an opportunity to prosper, if only because over the next decade it may become ever more valuable to those people who are looking for *voices that speak the truth to them about the things that they believe matter.*[8]

I believe Abrahamson has beautifully captured the power of magazines. But I also believe that with careful attention to recasting products such as newspapers and Web sites vis-à-vis the identity-based model of journalism, other media can be the mediators of shared interests, creators of community, and voices of truth for audiences.

Many industries are dealing with the concept of service in this era, some better than others, but most are struggling. One common negative example is the airline industry. Many major carriers have resorted to charging customers for services that used to be included in the price of a ticket: checking baggage, meals, even pillows. The financial service industry is faring even worse in the public's perception: lending less, charging more, and rewarding its already-rich executives. I often use examples such as these in my classes when I first introduce the concept of journalism as a service-oriented business. These are practices people easily understand because they have either travelled or invested money or followed the news about one or the other. It is my attempt to begin to establish the difference between this service-based way of thinking and the dated social responsibility approach to journalism.

But in offering this example, I learned something from an audience I had in front of me in early 2009. I asked a group of students what other service industries they could name. The first response: "education." For a noneducator this might not seem startling, but it shook me. I have shared this anecdote with colleagues, and all felt the same initial affront I did. Thankfully, I have had time to reflect on the perspective of education as a service-oriented business, and I have come to an understanding that might be relevant to our discussion here. To this student, education was a service-oriented business. He paid. He wanted something in return. In some classes he was satisfied, and in some he was not. To me, education claimed a place on a higher plane. It was about a faculty member, an expert, determining what mattered and teaching it to students in a way that was meaningful. Instead of my students' satisfaction I was concerned with their intellectual growth and their ability to provide evidence-based reasoning for their points of view. Light-blub moment: I was the "journalist." He was the "audience." And I was operating in a dated way of doing things, without thinking about the changes among today's students. If I thought about my students in the same way I encourage journalists to think about their audience, I would undoubtedly have more success. It is still my job to decide what is important and what should be in my course's syllabus, but it is also my job to engage students with the material. I now use different techniques in the classroom, and they are constantly evolving as I meet new students every term.

Journalists must also use new techniques. In fact, their task is even more pressing. Students who want to earn a degree have to take certain courses. There are limited options and a structured timeframe. But people who want news can get it from a variety of sources, which can mean abandoning some outlets and channels altogether. One of the real challenges to journalists in shifting from a social responsibility approach to an identity-based approach in their work is that it is actually more than a *shift*. Because they are so solidly grounded in the social responsibility mission, journalists tend to hear the identity-based model of journalism as I have conceptualized it as similar to the work they are doing now: serving people, just in a different way. From this perspective, they object to the identity-based model as being too much like marketing. But this objection misses the point entirely. The identity-based model is not a shift. It is a 360-degree turn. Here is another way to think about it: The social responsibility model of journalism provides that services come from the top down. Journalists in this model are the arbiters of what people should know, should read, and should care about. The identity-based model of journalism lets the audience have this power. To extend the parallel, it is a bottom-up model. The audience determines everything. Journalists have to fit the audience's mold. And if there is news that journalists think the audience needs to know, they have to figure out how to cast it in the audience's interest.

This raises the bar on what it means to be a journalist today. It demands that modern journalists deal with relevance. One story might have to be cast five different ways if the news organization serves five different audiences. The facts, the core of the narrative, may be the same, but the approaches, especially the lead and the presentation, are likely to vary widely. While news organizations need to determine on a community-by-community and audience-by-audience basis the best approach, we can consider some examples generally to advance our understanding of this idea of relevance. For instance, an audience we have previously called "public affairs junkies" may see value in a long narrative explanation with extensive sourcing, while having no need for the flashy, visual presentation of data. This type of public-affairs oriented audience likely favors official sources rather than person-on-the-street interviews. For them, the headline and the lead should be more serious. The same story might be recast for a mobile-driven, young, white-collar audience as only a headline and a two-sentence explanation of the implication of the story for the reader. A good example to consider in this context is road construction. The public affairs junkie craves context and depth. That might be related to local support and federal funding for the project, the construction companies who bid on the contract, how it was awarded, and the timeline for completion. The mobile professional wants to know how the construction impacts her drive home, period.

On top of expanding the skill set required to do the work of journalists today, there is another challenge that I have only begun to detect as I consider the identity- or audience-based approach. There is a potential misapprehension that many journalists encounter: *confusing audience with subject*. Let us explore this with a readily understood example. News organizations, newspapers especially, have been chasing what has been called the "elusive young reader." The hunt for 18- to 34-year-olds has been widely practiced for the past 15 years. Many publications designed for this audience have folded. Others have had commercial success as defined by circulation and advertising revenue, the traditional measures from the social responsibility model of journalism. But I believe that in many cases their impact—the new measure associated with the identity-based model of journalism—has waned because they have confused audience and subject. Young adults do not pick up news products to only read about young adults. They generally want news products that reflect their realities, yes, but their realities include a number of important topics such as taxes, rental or home ownership, commuting, health care, and professional or economic news. Instead, the majority of young-reader publications have chosen exclusively shallow topics—celebrities, dining and drinking, and sports. This has, in some cases, earned them business success but not social or political success.

A new model of journalism is key for modern theoretical research and journalism and educational practices if it is to have enduring strength as the journalism marketplace continues to shift at an accelerated pace. What is known for sure is the future of journalism is not here; it is ahead of us. It is continually ahead of us. The technology and the audience will continue to change. The purpose of adopting a new theoretical approach to understanding the relationships of media with their audiences is to equip students and practicing journalists with the concepts to continue to evolve with the changing media marketplace.

What we know is that journalism matters. The reporting and writing that determines what will become our nation's and our world's history matters. The checks on government, businesses, and other institutions by journalism matter. But all of these precepts do not matter simply because journalism exists. That is the dated position of the social responsibility model of journalism: that dissemination of news is paramount. Journalism matters when it has relevance, makes an impact, calls people to action, changes their beliefs or actions, or presents untold stories. This kind of journalism is a brave new world. It requires reinvention and innovation. It requires a new skill set for journalists: audience understanding. It requires attention to why people read, not just what they read. These are the principles of the identity-based model of journalism. Journalism matters only because people—their best interests, their livelihoods, their communities—matter.

Notes

CHAPTER 1: A BRAVE NEW WORLD OF JOURNALISM

1. Meyer, *The Vanishing Newspaper*, 7.
2. Stone, Stone, and Trotter, "Newspaper Quality's Relation to Circulation."
3. NAA, *Daily Newspaper Readership Trends*.
4. Sanoff, "TV News Growing Too Powerful?"
5. I believe there are many terms that can be used interchangeably for audience members although none is perfect. "Readers" implies a passive audience. "Users" suggests a consumption type not typically associated with information and is usually reserved for Web sites with a high level of interactivity. "Consumers" is widely used in marketing but still resisted in journalism circles. Other descriptors have been suggested: co-creators, partners, producers, and community members. I find these laden with their own problems and choose to rely on readers, users, and consumers with full recognition of their shortcomings.
6. Notably, the Tribune Company sold controlling ownership of the Chicago Cubs and the company's quarter interest in Comcast SportsNet (CSN) to the Ricketts family in 2009 for $845 million. Tribune retained a 5-percent ownership interest in the Cubs.
7. The First Amendment of the Bill of Rights guarantees five freedoms, among them, freedom of the press: "Congress shall make no law respecting an establishment of religion, or prohibiting the free exercise thereof; or abridging the freedom of speech, or of the press; or the right of the people peaceably to assemble, and to petition the government for a redress of grievances."
8. Kimball, "Gourmet to All That."
9. Ibid.
10. Watson, "Smile? Celebrity News Reaches Young Readers," 5.

11. Manjoo, "All the News Stuff That's Fit to Print."

12. Donatello, "Audience Research for Newspapers."

13. Fisher's three-part definition also included these two tenets: "news is what people need to know" and "news is a moneymaking proposition." Fisher, "News: A Three-Part Definition."

14. Madigan, "The Problem with Today's Journalism."

15. Pew Research Center, *Majorities Say Right Amount on Leadership and Policies*.

16. McCauley and Nesbitt, *Newspaper Experience Study*.

17. Peck and Malthouse, eds., *Medill on Media Engagement*.

18. Hodgins, "A Definition of News for the World of Tomorrow."

19. Meyer, "In Defense of the Marketing Approach."

20. Ibid., 60.

21. Wilkinson, "Role of Audiences."

22. Ibid.

23. Downie and Schudson, *The Reconstruction of American Journalism*, 75.

24. Briggs, "The End of Journalism as Usual."

CHAPTER 2: FROM WHENCE JOURNALISTS CAME

1. The quote can be originally attributed to Finley Peter Dunne who wrote as the fictional Mr. Dooley, the "author," from the late 1890s through the early part of the 20th century. It has been cut and revised since. In fact, a version was delivered by Gene Kelly (E. K. Hornbeck) in the 1960 film *Inherit the Wind*: "Mr. Brady, it is the duty of a newspaper to comfort the afflicted and afflict the comfortable."

2. Sherman, "Post Apocalypse."

3. Newseum, *Newseum Core Messages*.

4. Aeikens, "Our Profession Is Not Dying, It's Just Changing," 3.

5. Woodruff, "Are Journalists Obsolete?"

6. Wolff, "Post Modern."

7. Pew Research Center, *Social Networking and Online Videos Take Off*.

8. de Tocqueville, *Democracy in America*, 517–518.

9. ASNE, *Problems of Journalism: Proceedings*.

10. Commission on Freedom of the Press, *A Free and Responsible Press*.

11. Ibid., 21–29.

12. Siebert, Peterson, and Schramm, *Four Theories*, 74.

13. Ibid.

14. ASNE, *Statement of Principles*.

15. Carter, classroom discussion, UNC-Chapel Hill.

16. Doogan, "The Exit Interview."

17. Harris, "Jay Harris' Speech to ASNE."

18. For up-to-date ownership lists, see *Columbia Journalism Review*'s *Who Owns What* database, http://www.cjr.org/resources/index.php?c=american (accessed November 1, 2009).

19. Picard, "Commercialism and Newspaper Quality," 54.

20. Rosen, *What Are Journalists For?* 20–21.

21. Stepp, "Journalism without Profit Margins," 38.

22. Lewis, "The Nonprofit Road," 36.

23. Meyer, *The Vanishing Newspaper*, 9.

24. Ibid., 10.

25. C-SPAN, "Future of Journalism and Newspapers."

26. Disclosure: Since May 2008, I have served as an advisory member of the Knight Commission on the Information Needs of Communities in a Democracy, jointly organized by the John S. and James L. Knight Foundation and the Aspen Institute.

27. Curley, "It's about the News," 25.

CHAPTER 3: AUDIENCE NEEDS AND ACTIONS

1. Herzog, "On Borrowed Experience." Lazarsfeld and Stanton, eds., *Radio Research, 1941*. Lazarsfeld and Stanton, eds., *Radio Research, 1942–1943*. Herzog was the second wife of Paul Lazarsfeld but eventually married and became Herzog-Massing.

2. *Time*, "Radio: Why Do They Like It?"

3. Wolf and Fiske, "The Children Talk about Comics."

4. Berelson, "What 'Missing the Newspaper' Means."

5. Katz, Gurevitch, and Haas, "On the Use of the Mass Media."

6. Ibid., 179.

7. Bogart, *Press and Public*.

8. Jeffres and Atkin, "Dimensions of Student Interest."

9. Collins, "Level of On-Campus Activities Predicts Student Paper Readership."

10. Thurlow and Milo, "Newspaper Readership: Can the Bleeding Be Stopped?"

11. Beaudoin and Thorson, "A Marketplace Theory."

12. Albarran et al., "'What Happened to Our Audience?'"

13. Larkin and Grotta, "The Newspaper as a Source of Consumer Information."

14. Barnhurst and Wartella, "Newspapers and Citizenship."

15. Ibid., 195.

16. NAA changed its reporting procedure in 2008 to focus on the characteristics of readers as opposed to detailing who read—and therefore who did not. For full 2008 report, see NAA, *2008 Daily Newspaper Section Readership Report*.

17. Rubin et al., "Media Use and Meaning of Music Video."

18. Austin, "Motivations for Movie Attendance."

19. Tewksbury and Althaus, "An Examination of Motivations for Using the World Wide Web."

20. Urista, Qingwne, and Day, "Explaining Why Young Adults Use MySpace and Facebook."

21. Haridakis and Hanson, "Social Interaction and Co-Viewing with You Tube."

22. Barton, "Reality Television Programming and Diverging Gratifications."

23. Vincent and Basil, "College Students' News Gratifications."

24. McCauley and Nesbitt, *Newspaper Experience Study*.

25. Nesbitt and Lavine, *Reaching New Readers*.

26. Nesbitt and Lavine, *Reinventing the Newspaper Young Adults*. This work was before the paper filed for bankruptcy under the ownership of Avista Capital Partners.

27. Peer et al., *Local TV News Experience*.

28. Peer, *User Engagement Study*.

29. MMC, ASME, and MPA, *Highlights from the Magazine Reader Experience Study*.

30. Peck and Malthouse, *Medill on Media Engagement*.

31. Mersey, "The Identity Experience."

32. NEA, *To Read or Not to Read*.

33. Among the four groups 45 years old and older, the change was not statistically significant.

34. Master, "Media Insiders Say Internet Hurts Journalism." Respondents to the *Atlantic/National Journal* Media Insider's Poll: Peter Beinart, Gloria Borger, David Brooks, Carl Cannon, Tucker Carlson, Jonathan Chait, Roger Cohen, Steve Coll, Sam Donaldson, Bob Edwards, James Fallows, Howard Fineman, Frank Foer, Ron Fournier, Jeffrey Goldberg, Jeff Greenfield, Glenn Greenwald, David Gregory, Mark Halperin, Christopher Hitchens, Al Hunt, Mort Kondracke, Jim Lehrer, Ruth Marcus, Joshua Micah Marshall, Chris Matthews, Jane Mayer, Doyle McManus, John Micklethwait, Dana Milbank, Markos Moulitsas, Katherine McIntire Peters, Todd Purdum, Cokie Roberts, Eugene Robinson, Tom Shoop, Roger Simon, Scott Simon, Ray Suarez, Nina Totenberg, Linda Wertheimer, Leon Wieseltier, Juan Williams, Judy Woodruff, and Fareed Zakaria.

35. Lipset and Schneider, *The Confidence Gap*.

36. Pew Research Center, *Who Moves?*

CHAPTER 4: WHY THE AUDIENCE DOES WHAT IT DOES

1. Picard, "Money, Media, and the Public Interest," 346.

2. Bulkeley, *Corporate Seers*.

3. Mersey, "Online News Users' Sense of Community."

4. Jeffres et al., "Newspaper Reading Supports Community Involvement."

5. See most recent report, Project for Excellence in Journalism, *State of the News Media: 2009*. See index of reports, 2005–2009, http://www.journalism.org/ (accessed November 11, 2009).

6. Roberts, "Ebony: Up for Sale?"

7. Cover, "Engaging Sexualities."

8. Park, "Urbanization as Measured by Newspaper Circulation."

9. Ibid., 75.

10. Merton, "Patterns of Influence."

11. Stamm, *Community Ties and Newspaper Use*, 8.

12. Mersey, "Sense of Community Differs for Print, Online Readers."

13. Hillery, "Definitions of Community."

14. Chavis and Newbrough, "The Meaning of 'Community,'" 335.

15. Johnson, *Emergence*, 106–107.

16. Facebook, "Statistics."

17. Barabási, *Linked*.

18. Milgram, "The Small-World Problem."

19. Ahmed, "The 50 Most Popular Celebs on Twitter."

20. Sarason, *The Psychological Sense of Community*, 156–157.

21. McMillan and Chavis, "Sense of Community," 9.

22. Ibid.

23. Ibid.

24. Ibid., 14.

25. Chavis et al., "Sense of Community through Brunswik's Lens."

26. For more on the SCI, see Perkins et al., "Participation and the Social and Physical Environment." The SCI is a 12-item measure designed for true/false responses: (1) I think my block is a good place for me to live. (2) People on this block do not share the same values. (3) My neighbors and I want the same things from the block. (4) I can recognize most people who live on my block. (5) I feel at home on this block. (6) Very few of my neighbors know me. (7) I care about what my neighbors think of my actions. (8) I have almost no influence over what this block is like. (9) If there is a problem on this block, people who live here can get it solved. (10) It is very important to me to live on this particular block. (11) People on this block generally don't get along with each other. (12) I expect to live on this block for a long time.

27. Greer, "Psychological and Support Functions of an E-mail Mailing List."

28. Boyd, "In Community We Trust."

29. Blanchard, "Blogs as Virtual Communities."

30. Tajfel, "Social Identity and Intergroup Behavior," 69.

31. Harwood, "Viewing Age," 204.

32. Bakagiannis and Tarrant, "Can Music Bring People Together?" 129.

33. Price, "Social Identification and Public Opinion," 201.

34. Harwood, "Age Identification."

35. Ruggiero and Yang, "Latino Ethnic Identity."

36. The Classical Music Consumer Segmentation Study highlighted here was part of the Foundation's decade-long, $10 million Magic of Music initiative. The study, conducted by Audience Insight LLC of Southport, Conn., was done in partnership with 15 American orchestras and comprised more than 25,000 interviews. Access reports from the study online at http://www.knightfdn.org/research_publications/ (accessed January 27, 2009). The data are archived in full at the UNC-Chapel Hill's Odum Institute, http://www.irss.unc.edu/odum/jsp/home.jsp.

37. McPhee, *Bridging the Gap: Orchestra and Community*, 3.

38. Ibid., 4.

39. Ibid., 3.

CHAPTER 5: THE AUDIENCE ALREADY HAS CONTROL

1. Kimball, "Gourmet to All That."

2. *Cooks*.com, "Terms of Usage."

3. The *Washington Post* published its last edition of its review section, Book World, in February 2009.

4. Heys, "A Second Look at New Models."

5. See http://epaper.aztrib.com/ (accessed November 18, 2009).

6. *Washington Post*, "The *Washington Post* Launches Facebook Connect."

7. CNN, "About CNN iReport."

8. YouTube also created News Near You, a feature that identifies a user's location and aggregates relevant local videos for him or her. YouTube has invited more than 25,000 news sources to participate in this program by supplying video. ABC News, the Associated Press, and Reuters have all accepted.

9. Miller and Stone, "'Hyperlocal' Web Sites Deliver News."

10. Buttry, "Roles Change as the *Gazette* Changes."

11. NAA, "Newspaper Web Sites Expand Reach."

12. NAA, "Newspaper Web Sites Attract 74 Million Visitors."

13. Pew Internet and American Life Project, "Online News."

14. Horrigan, "Home Broadband Adoption 2009."

15. PEJ, *The State of News Media 2006*.

16. NAA, "Interactive Media."

17. USC Annenberg News, "Annual Internet Survey by Center for the Digital Future."

18. AP, *A New Model for News*.

19. Ibid., 43.

20. Heys, "Lee Study Shows Audience Growth."

21. Palser, "News à la Carte."

22. Curtain, Dougall, and Mersey, "Study Compares Yahoo! News Story Preferences," 32.

23. Schaefer, "DigitalNext: Facebook Connect."

24. Humphreys, "Co-producing Experiences."

25. NPR, "Comments on Comments."

26. For results, see PEJ, *The State of the News Media 2008*; PEJ, *The State of the News Media 2009*.

27. Walsh, "Nielsen: Smartphones to Be Majority of Cell Phones."

CHAPTER 6: A NEW FRAMEWORK

1. The *Miami Herald* still announced in December 2009 that it was cutting 24 jobs and reducing the hours of workers involved in printing and delivering the paper. It already cut more than 190 jobs in two rounds in 2009. In 2008, the *Herald* eliminated more than 370 jobs.

2. Nicolosi, "Executive Producer Michelle Nicolosi Talks."

3. Pérez-Peña, "Seattle Paper Is Resurgent as a Solo Act."

4. Burghart, "The Coming Golden Age of Journalism."

5. Levitt, "Best of *HBR* 1960: Marketing Myopia," 2.

6. Ibid., 3.

7. Lowry, "Can This Man Save AOL?" 43.

8. Ibid., 44.

9. "The Grave Dancer's Folly," 4.

10. Nordenson, "Overload!" 30.

11. Sifry, "A See-through Society."

12. Ibid., 43.

13. Lenhart, "The Democratization of Online Social Networks." Research from the Pew Research Center has also revealed that socioeconomic stratification observed among off-line participatory activities is also present online. That is income and education are highly correlated with online political activity. For more, see Smith et al., *The Internet and Civic Engagement.*

14. Nordenson, "Overload!" 30.

15. Schmidt, "How Google Can Help Save Newspapers."

16. Tajfel, "Social Identity and Intergroup Behavior," 72.

17. In 2005, the largest 200 newspapers by count were fewer than 15 percent of all U.S. dailies, but they accounted for more than 80 percent of total circulation. The top-200 limit corresponded roughly to newspapers with average daily circulation of 50,000 or more.

18. The Gini coefficient based on the 2005 circulation penetration also had a minimum of 0.092, a maximum of 0.647, and a standard deviation of 0.077.

19. Wolcott, "What's a Culture Snob to Do?" 68.

20. Purdum, "It Came from Wasilla."

21. Lewis, "The Man Who Crashed the World."

22. Munk, "Rich Harvard, Poor Harvard."

23. Mersey, "The Identity Experience."

24. *RealClearPolitics*.com, "*RealClearPolitics*.com Launches."

CHAPTER 7: PAYING FOR IT ALL

1. We know from examples such as the *Los Angeles Times'* special editorial section on the Staples Center for which the arena and newspaper had a profit-sharing agreement that the wall was not so impervious, but attention to these ethical issues is outside the scope of this book.

2. Gilson, "Black and White and Dead All Over."

3. Arends, "Will the News Survive?"

4. Gilson, "Black and White and Dead All Over."

5. TimesSelect was free to print subscribers. For others, it was $49.95 a year or $7.95 a month.

6. Pérez-Peña, "Times to Stop Charging for Parts of Its Web Site."

7. Ibid.

8. Pérez-Peña and Arango, "They Pay for Cable, Music and Extra Bags."

9. Ibid.

10. Ibid.

11. *MinnPost*.com, "About Us."

12. *Miami Herald*, "Support Ongoing News Coverage."

13. Moore, "Can a Customized Paper Survive the Demise of Print?"

14. Yuan, "Mort Zuckerman's Plan to Save Newspapers."

15. See video at http://www.youtube.com/watch?v=2kvEgeC-nAk (accessed December 13, 2009).

16. Manjoo, "The *Wall Street Journal's* Web Site Is Already (Secretly) Free."

17. Wilkinson, "Content's Monetary Value Determined by Content."

18. Loayza, "5 Business Models for Social Media Startups."

19. As an added revenue opportunity, Facebook added the functionality in 2009 to uses its Gift Store to also buy real gifts to send to Facebook friends.

20. Shapira, "The Death of Journalism."

21. Ibid.

22. Osnos, "What's a Fair Share in the Age of Google?"

23. Ibid., 25.

24. Ibid.

25. Farhi, "Build That Pay Wall High."

26. American Press Institute, *Online Revenue Initiatives 2009*.

27. Pérez-Peña, "About Half in U.S. Would Pay."

28. Boston Consulting Group, "News for Sale."

29. Mersey, Malthouse, and Calder, "Engagement with Online Media."

30. Association of National Advertisers, "Engagement, Brand Idea and Consumer Insight."

31. Calder, Malthouse, and Schaedel, "Engagement with Online Media and Advertising Effectiveness." Calder and Malthouse, "Media Engagement and Advertising Effectiveness." Calder and Malthouse, "Media Brands and Integrated Marketing."

32. Wetpaint and Altimeter, *The World's Most Valuable Brands*.

33. Ibid.

34. Kiley, "Paying for Viewers."

35. In 2008 Nielsen purchased IAG, the research firm that began recall studies in 2004, for $225 million.

36. Ibid.

37. Collins and Armstrong, "U of Florida Students Prefer Campus Paper."

38. Meyer, "The Elite Newspaper of the Future."

39. Pinch Media, "Paid Applications on the App Store."

40. Knee, Greenwald, and Seave, "All (Profitable) Media Is Local," 187.

41. Ibid.

CHAPTER 8: JOURNALISM IS SPELLED WITH AN "I"

1. Zeeck, "ASNE President's Speech." In 2009 members of ASNE voted to rename the organization the American Society of News Editors.

2. PEJ, "Introduction," *The State of the News Media 2009*.

3. *Washington Post,* "Correction."
4. Rosenberg, "The Post's Public Enemy Gaffe."
5. Pérez-Peña, "Why Big Newspapers Applaud Some Declines."
6. Leadingham, "10: David Cohn," 14.
7. Abrahamson, "The Future of Magazines."
8. Ibid.

Bibliography

Abrahamson, David. "The Future of Magazines, 2010–2020." *Journalism of Magazine and New Media Research* 10, no. 2 (Spring 2009): http://aejmcmagazine. asu.edu/Journal/Spring2009/Abrahamson.pdf (accessed January 18, 2010).

Aeikens, Dave. "Our Profession Is Not Dying, It's Just Changing." *Quill*, December 2008, 3.

Ahmed, Murad. "The 50 Most Popular Celebs on Twitter." *Times Online*, February 2, 2009: http://technology.timesonline.co.uk/tol/news/tech_and_web/article5641893.ece (accessed November 19, 2009).

Albarran, Alan B., Tonya Anderson, Ligia Garcia Bejar, Anna L. Bussart, Elizabeth Daggett, Sarah Gibson, Matt Gorman, Danny Greer, Miao Guo, Jennifer L. Horst, Tania Khalaf, John Phillip Lay, Michael McCracken, Bill Mott, and Heather Way. "'What Happened to Our Audience?' Radio and New Technology Uses and Gratifications among Young Adult Users." *Journal of Radio Studies* 14, no. 2 (2007): 92–101.

American Press Institute. *Online Revenue Initiatives 2009*. Reston, VA: API, November 2009: http://www.newspapernext.org/OnlineRev2009FINAL.pdf (accessed December 8, 2009).

American Society of Newspaper Editors. *Problems of Journalism: Proceedings of the First Annual Meeting, Society of Newspaper Editors*. Washington, D.C.: ASNE, April 27–28, 1923.

———. *Statement of Principles*, 1975: http://asne.org/article_view/smid/370/articleid/325/reftab/79/t/asnes-statement-of-principles.aspx (accessed March 6, 2007).

Arends, Brett. "Will the News Survive?" *Market Watch*, December 8, 2009: http://www.marketwatch.com/story/will-the-news-survive-2009-12-08 (accessed December 8, 2009).

Associated Press. *A New Model for News: Studying the Deep Structure of Young-Adult News Consumption.* New York: AP, June 2008.

Association of National Advertisers. "Engagement, Brand Idea and Consumer Insight." *ANA Marketing Maestros* (September 26, 2006): http://ana.blogs.com/maestros/2006/09/the_engagement_.html (accessed December 16, 2009).

Austin, Bruce A. "Motivations for Movie Attendance." *Communication Quarterly* 34, no. 2 (Spring 1986): 115–126.

Bakagiannis, Sotirios, and Mark Tarrant. "Can Music Bring People Together? Effects of Shared Musical Preference on Intergroup Bias in Adolescence." *Scandinavian Journal of Psychology* 47 (2006): 129–136.

Barabási, Albert-Lászió. *Linked: How Everything Is Connected to Everything Else and What It Means for Business, Science, and Everyday Life.* New York: Plume, 2002.

Barnhurst, Kevin G., and Ellen Wartella. "Newspapers and Citizenship: Young Adults' Subjective Experience of Newspapers." *Critical Studies in Mass Communication* 8 (1991): 195–209.

Barton, Kristin M. "Reality Television Programming and Diverging Gratifications: The Influence of Content on Gratifications Obtained." *Journal of Broadcasting & Electronic Media* 53, no. 3 (2009): 460–476.

Beaudoin, Christopher E., and Ester Thorson. "A Marketplace Theory of Media Use." *Mass Communication & Society* 5, no. 3 (2002): 241–262.

Berelson, Bernard. "What 'Missing the Newspaper' Means." In *Communications Research*, edited by Paul F. Lazarsfeld and Frank N. Stanton, 111–129. New York: Harper & Brothers, 1949.

Blanchard, Anita. "Blogs as Virtual Communities: Identifying a Sense of Community in the Julie/Julia Project." *Into the Blogosphere: Rhetoric, Community, and the Culture of Weblogs:* http://blog.lib.umn.edu/blogosphere/blogs_as_virtual.html (accessed August 10, 2006).

Bogart, Leo. *Press and Public: Who Reads What, When, Where and Why in American Newspapers.* 2nd ed. Hillsdale, NJ: Lawrence Erlbaum Associates, 1989.

Boston Consulting Group. "News for Sale: Charges for Online News Are Set to Become the Norm as Most Consumers Say They Are Willing to Pay, According to The Boston Consulting Group." News release, November 16, 2009: http://www.bcg.com/media/PressReleaseDetails.aspx?id=tcm:12-35297 (accessed November 16, 2009).

Boyd, Josh. "In Community We Trust: Online Security Communication at eBay." *Journal of Computer-Mediated Communication* 7, no. 3 (April 2002): http://jcmc.indiana.edu/vol7/issue3/boyd.html (accessed October 12, 2006).

Briggs, Mark. "The End of Journalism as Usual." *Nieman Reports* (Winter 2008): http://www.nieman.harvard.edu/reportsitem.aspx?id=100689 (accessed January 19, 2010).

Bulkeley, William M. "Corporate Seers: Who Knows Better What the Future Holds Than Those Who Make a Living Thinking about It?" *Wall Street Journal*, November 16, 1998: R37.

Burghart, D. Brian. "The Coming Golden Age of Journalism: One Editor's Analysis of and Hopes for the Future of the Printed Word." *Reno News & Review*, February 19, 2009: http://www.newsreview.com/reno/content?oid=914453 (accessed October 26, 2009).

Buttry, Steve. "Roles Change as the Gazette Changes." *Pursuing the Complete Community Connection*, March 8, 2009: http://stevebuttry.wordpress.com/2009/03/08/roles-change-as-the-gazette-changes/ (accessed November 29, 2009).

C-SPAN. "Future of Journalism and Newspapers." *C-SPAN*, May 6, 2009: http://www.c-spanarchives.org/library/includes/templates/library/flash_popup.php?pID=285745-1&clipStart=&clipStop= (accessed July 13, 2009).

Calder, Bobby J., and Edward C. Malthouse. "Media Brands and Integrated Marketing." In *Media Brands and Branding*, edited by Mart Ots, 89–94. Media Management and Transformation Centre, JIBS Research Report No. 2008-1, 2008.

Calder, Bobby J., and Edward C. Malthouse. "Media Engagement and Advertising Effectiveness." In *Kellogg on Media and Advertising*, edited by Bobby J. Calder, 1–36. New York: Wiley, 2008.

Calder, Bobby J., Edward C. Malthouse, and Ute Schaedel. "Engagement with Online Media and Advertising Effectiveness." *Journal of Interactive Marketing* 23, no. 4 (2009): 321–331.

Carter, Hodding, III. (class discussion, University of North Carolina at Chapel Hill, Chapel Hill, NC, March 2006).

Chavis, David M., and J. R. Newbrough. "The Meaning of 'Community' in Community Psychology." *Journal of Community Psychology* 14, no. 4 (October 1986): 335–340.

Chavis, David M., James H. Hogge, David W. McMillan, and Abraham Wandersman. "Sense of Community through Brunswik's Lens: A First Look." *Journal of Community Psychology* 14 (January 1986): 24–40.

CNN. "About CNN iReport." *CNN*.com: http://www.ireport.com/about.jspa (accessed November 18, 2009).

Collins, Steve J. "Level of On-Campus Activities Predicts Student Paper Readership." *Newspaper Research Journal* 24, no. 4 (2003): 102–105.

Collins, Steve J., and Cory L. Armstrong. "U of Florida Students Prefer Campus Paper to Free Daily." *Newspaper Research Journal* 29, no. 1 (2008): 77–89.

Columbia Journalism Review. Who Owns What: http://www.cjr.org/resources/index.php?c=american (accessed November 1, 2009).

Commission on Freedom of the Press. *A Free and Responsible Press: A General Report on Mass Communication*, edited by Robert D. Leigh. Chicago: University of Chicago Press, 1974.

Cooks.com. "Terms of Usage." *Privacy Statement*: http://www.cooks.com/rec/privacy.html (accessed November 17, 2009).

Cover, Rob. "Engaging Sexualities: Lesbian/Gay Print Journalism, Community Belonging, Social Space and Physical Place." *Pacific Journalism Review* 11, no. 1 (2005): 113–132.

Curley, Rob. "It's about the News, Not the Paper." *The Journalist* (2007): 23–35.

Curtain, Patricia A., Elizabeth Dougall, and Rachel Davis Mersey. "Study Compares Yahoo! News Story Preferences." *Newspaper Research Journal* 28, no. 4 (Fall 2007): 22–35.

de Tocqueville, Alexis. *Democracy in America.* Republication edited by K. P. Mayer and Max Lerner and translated by George Lawrence. New York: Harper & Row, 1996: 517–518.

Donatello, Michael C. "Audience Research for Newspapers: Newspapers Seek to Tailor Products to Audiences." In *History of the Mass Media in the United States: An Encyclopedia,* edited by Margaret A. Blanchard, 51–53. Chicago: Fitzroy Dearborn, 1998.

Doogan, Mike. "The Exit Interview." *PoynterOnline,* January 26, 2004: http://www.poynter.org/content/content_view.asp?id=59894 (accessed October 23, 2006).

Downie, Leonard, Jr., and Michael Schudson. *The Reconstruction of American Journalism.* New York: Columbia University, October 19, 2009: http://www.journalism.columbia.edu/cs/ContentServer/jrn/1212611716674/page/1212611716651/JRNSimplePage2.htm (accessed December 3, 2009).

Facebook. "Statistics": http://www.facebook.com/press/info.php?statistics (accessed November 10, 2009).

Farhi, Paul. "Build That Pay Wall High." *American Journalism Review* (June/July 2009): http://www.ajr.org/Article.asp?id=4813 (accessed August 27, 2009).

Fisher, Charles N. "News: A Three-Part Definition." *Journalism Educator* 32, no. 2 (July 1977): 38.

Gilson, Dave. "Black and White and Dead All Over." *Mother Jones* (July/August 2009): http://motherjones.com/media/2009/07/black-and-white-and-dead-all-over (accessed August 27, 2009).

"The Grave Dancer's Folly: Blaming Newspapers for Their Plight Is a Waste of Precious Time." *Columbia Journalism Review* (July/August 2009): 4.

Greer, Bobby G. "Psychological and Support Functions of an E-mail Mailing List for Persons with Cerebral Palsy." *CyberPsychology & Behavior* 3, no. 2 (2000): 221–235.

Haridakis, Paul, and Gary Hanson. "Social Interaction and Co-Viewing with YouTube: Blending Mass Communication Reception and Social Connection." *Journal of Broadcasting & Electronic Media* 53, no. 2 (April 2009): 317–335.

Harris, Jay. "Jay Harris' Speech to ASNE." *PoynterOnline,* April 8, 2001: http://www.poynter.org/content/content_view.asp?id=4109&sid=14 (accessed April 15, 2010).

Harwood, Jake. "Viewing Age: Lifespan Identity and Television Viewing Choices." *Journal of Broadcasting & Electronic Media* 41 (Spring 1997): 203–213.

———. "Age Identification, Social Identity Gratifications, and Television Viewing." *Journal of Broadcasting & Electronic Media* 43, no. 1 (Winter 1999): 123–136.

Herzog, Herta. "On Borrowed Experience: An Analysis of Listening to Daytime Sketches." *Students in Philosophy and Social Science* 9, no. 1 (1941): 65–95.

Heys, John. "A Second Look at New Models: Newspapers' Business Practices Continue to Evolve." *Presstime* (December 2008): 18.

———. "Lee Study Shows Audience Growth across Platforms." *Presstime* (December 2008): 21.

Hillery, George A. "Definitions of Community: Areas of Agreement." *Rural Sociology* 20 (1955): 111–123.

Hodgins, Eric. "A Definition of News for the World of Tomorrow." *Journalism Quarterly* 20, no. 4 (December 1943): 275–276.

Horrigan, John. "Home Broadband Adoption 2009." *Pew Internet and American Life Project:* http://www.pewinternet.org/Reports/2009/10-Home-Broadband-Adoption-2009.aspx (accessed November 17, 2009).

Humphreys, Ashlee. "Co-producing Experiences." Chap. 9 in *Medill on Media Engagement*, edited by Abe Peck and Edward C. Malthouse. Cresskill, NJ: Hampton Press, forthcoming.

Jeffres, Leo W., and David J. Atkin. "Dimensions of Student Interest in Reading Newspapers." *Journalism & Mass Communication Educator* (Autumn 1996): 15–23.

Jeffres, Leo W., Jae-woo Lee, Kimberly Neuendorf, and David Atkin. "Newspaper Reading Supports Community Involvement." *Newspaper Research Journal* 28, no. 1 (Winter 2007): 6–23.

Johnson, Steven. *Emergence: The Connected Lives of Ants, Brains, Cities, and Software*. New York: Scribner, 2001.

Katz, Elihu, Michael Gurevitch, and Hadassah Haas. "On the Use of the Mass Media for Important Things." *American Sociological Review* 38 (1973): 164–181.

Kiley, David. "Paying for Viewers Who Pay Attention: Engagement Scores Are Helping TV Advertisers Target Ideal Audiences—Those Who Are Really Interested." *BusinessWeek* (May 18, 2009): 56.

Kimball, Christopher. "Gourmet to All That." *New York Times*, October 8, 2009: http://www.nytimes.com/2009/10/08/opinion/08kimball.html (accessed October 8, 2009).

Knee, Jonathan A., Bruce C. Greenwald, and Ava Seave. "All (Profitable) Media Is Local: Newspapers, Theaters, and Communications." Chap. 10 in *The Curse of the Mogul: What's Wrong with the World's Leading Media Companies*. New York: Portfolio, 2009.

Larkin, Ernest F., and Gerald L. Grotta. "The Newspaper as a Source of Consumer Information for Young Adults." *Journal of Advertising* 6, no. 4 (Fall 1977): 5–10.

Lazarsfeld, Paul F., and Frank N. Stanton, eds. *Radio Research, 1941*. New York: Duell, Sloan & Pearce, 1942.

Lazarsfeld, Paul F., and Frank N. Stanton, eds. *Radio Research, 1942–1943*. New York: Arno Press, 1944.

Leadingham, Scott. "10: David Cohn." *Quill*, August 2009, 14–15.

Lenhart, Amanda. "The Democratization of Online Social Networks." Presentation, AoIR 10.0, Milwaukee, WI, October 8, 2009: http://pewinternet.org/Presentations/2009/41—The-Democratization-of-Online-Social-Networks.aspx (accessed December 6, 2009).

Levitt, Theodore. "Best of *HBR* 1960: Marketing Myopia." *Harvard Business Review* (July/August 2004).

Lewis, Charles. "The Nonprofit Road: It's Paved Not with Gold, but with Good Journalism." *Columbia Journalism Review* (September/October 2007): 32–36: http://www.cjr.org/feature/the_nonprofit_road.php (accessed January 27, 2010).

Lewis, Michael. "The Man Who Crashed the World." *Vanity Fair*, August 2009, 98–103, 136–139.

Lipset, Seymour Martin, and William Schneider. *The Confidence Gap: Business, Labor, and Government in the Public Mind*. Revised ed. Baltimore, MD: Johns Hopkins University Press, 1987.

Loayza, Jun. "5 Business Models for Social Media Startups." *Mashable*.com, July 14, 2009: http://mashable.com/2009/07/14/social-media-business-models/ (accessed December 8, 2009).

Lowry, Tom. "Can This Man Save AOL?" *BusinessWeek* (December 14, 2009): 42–46.

Madigan, Charles M. "The Problem with Today's Journalism." *Chicago Tribune*, October 25, 2005: http://articles.chicagotribune.com/2005-10-25/news/0510250027_1_journalism-propaganda-daily-show (accessed April 15, 2010).

Manjoo, Farhad. "All the News Stuff That's Fit to Print: Facing a Slow Death, Newspapers Are Desperately Trying to Reach Young Readers with Dumbed-Down Tabloids Full of Stories about Kobe, Britney and Dental Bling." *Salon*.com, February 17, 2006: http://www.salon.com/news/feature/2006/02/17/newspapers/ (accessed February 28, 2006).

———. "The *Wall Street Journal*'s Web Site Is Already (Secretly) Free." *Salon*.com, March 21, 2008: http://machinist.salon.com/tech/machinist/blog/2008/03/21/wsj (accessed December 14, 2009).

Master, Cyra. "Media Insiders Say Internet Hurts Journalism." *Atlantic*, April 10, 2009: http://www.theatlantic.com/doc/200904u/media-insiders (accessed November 7, 2009).

McCauley, Todd, and Mary Nesbitt. *Newspaper Experience Study*. Evanston, IL: Readership Institute, May 2003: http://www.readership.org/consumers/data/newspaper_exp.pdf (accessed November 13, 2008).

McMillan, David W., and David M. Chavis. "Sense of Community: A Definition and Theory." *Journal of Community Psychology* 14 (January 1986): 9–14.

McPhee, Penelope. *Bridging the Gap: Orchestra and Community*. Issue brief 1. Miami: John S. and James L. Knight Foundation, 2002: http://www.knightfoundation.org/dotAsset/131781.pdf (accessed January 27, 2010).

Media Management Center, American Society of Magazine Editors, and Maga-
    zine Publishers of America. *Highlights from the Magazine Reader Experience
    Study*. Evanston, IL: Media Management Center, 2003: http://www.media
    managementcenter.org/research/magazineexperience.pdf (accessed June 9,
    2009).

Mersey, Rachel Davis. "Online News Users' Sense of Community: Is Geography
    Dead?" *Journalism Practice* 3, no. 3 (2009): 347–360.

———. "Sense of Community Differs for Print, Online Readers." *Newspaper Re-
    search Journal* 30, no. 3 (2009): 105–119.

———. "The Identity Experience." Chap. 8 in *Medill on Media Engagement*, ed-
    ited by Abe Peck and Edward C. Malthouse. Cresskill, NJ: Hampton Press,
    forthcoming.

Mersey, Rachel Davis, Edward C. Malthouse, and Bobby J. Calder. "Engagement
    with Online Media." *Journal of Media Business Studies* 7, no. 2 (forth-
    coming).

Merton, Robert. "Patterns of Influence: A Study of Interpersonal Influences and
    of Communications Behavior in a Local Community." In *Communications
    Research*, edited by Paul F. Lazarsfeld and Frank N. Stanton, 180–215. New
    York: Harper and Brothers, 1949.

Meyer, Philip. "In Defense of the Marketing Approach." *Columbia Journalism Re-
    view* (January/February 1978): 60–62.

———. *The Vanishing Newspaper: Saving Journalism in the Information Age*. Co-
    lumbia: University of Missouri Press, 2004.

———. "The Elite Newspaper of the Future." *American Journalism Review* (Oc-
    tober/November 2008): http://www.ajr.org/Article.asp?id=4605 (accessed
    November 8, 2009).

Miami Herald. "Support Ongoing News Coverage." *MiamiHerald*.com: https://
    extra.herald.com/events/CustomerInfo.aspx?EventId=8&ProductId=28
    (accessed January 28, 2010).

Milgram, Stanley. "The Small-World Problem." *Psychology Today* 1, no. 1 (1967):
    60–67.

Miller, Claire Cain, and Brad Stone. "'Hyperlocal' Web Sites Deliver News with-
    out Newspapers." *New York Times*, April 13, 2009: http://www.nytimes.com/
    2009/04/13/technology/start-ups/13hyperlocal.html (accessed November 17,
    2009).

MinnPost.com. "About Us." *MinnPost*.com: http://www.minnpost.com/about/ (ac-
    cessed October 2, 2009).

Moore, Tristana. "Can a Customized Paper Survive the Demise of Print?" *Time*,
    October 23, 2009: http://www.time.com/time/business/article/0,8599,
    1931356,00.html (accessed October 25, 2009).

Munk, Nina. "Rich Harvard, Poor Harvard." *Vanity Fair*, August 2009, 106–112,
    144–148.

National Endowment for the Arts. *To Read or Not to Read: A Question of National
    Consequence*. Washington, D.C.: NEA, 2007:http://www.nea.gov/research/
    ToRead.pdf (accessed November 7, 2009).

National Public Radio. "Comments on Comments." *On the Media*, July 25, 2008: http://www.onthemedia.org/transcripts/2008/07/25/03 (accessed November 29, 2009).

Nesbitt, Mary, and John Lavine. *Reaching New Readers: Revolution, not Evolution.* Evanston, IL: Readership Institute, July 2004: http://www.readership.org/new_readers/data/overview.pdf (accessed August 3, 2009).

Nesbitt, Mary, and John Lavine. *Reinventing the Newspaper Young Adults: A Joint Project of the Readership Institute and* Star Tribune. Evanston, IL: Readership Institute, April 2005: http://www.readership.org/experience/startrib_overview.pdf (accessed August 3, 2009).

Newseum. *Newseum Core Messages:* http://www.newseum.org/about/overview/about.aspx?item=coreMessages&style=b (accessed October 29, 2009).

Newspaper Association of America. "Newspaper Web Sites Expand Reach of Total Newspaper Audience, According to Latest Newspaper Audience Database." News release, June 13, 2007: http://www.naa.org/PressCenter/SearchPressReleases/2006/NEWSPAPER-WEB-SITES-EXPAND-REACH-OF-TOTAL-NEWSPAPER-AUDIENCE.aspx (accessed January 27, 2010).

———. *2008 Daily Newspaper Section Readership Report:* http://www.naa.org/docs/Research/Daily-Readership-Active.pdf (accessed November 6, 2009).

———. "Newspaper Web Sites Attract 74 Million Visitors in Third Quarter as Industry Grows Audience across Multiple Platforms." News release, October 22, 2009: http://www.naa.org/PressCenter/SearchPressReleases/2009/NEWSPAPER-WEB-SITES-ATTRACT-74-MILLION-VISITORS-IN-THIRD-QUARTER.aspx (accessed November 17, 2009).

———. "Interactive Media: Extending the Franchise": http://www.naa.org/thesource/23.asp (accessed October 9, 2006).

———. *Daily Newspaper Readership Trends:* http://www.naa.org/TrendsandNumbers/Readership.aspx (accessed October 18, 2009).

Nicolosi, Michelle. "Executive Producer Michelle Nicolosi Talks about the New *SeattlePI.com*." *SeattlePI.com*, March 16, 2009: http://www.seattlepi.com/business/403794_newseattlepi.com16.html (accessed August 11, 2009).

Nordenson, Bree. "Overload! Journalism's Battle for Relevance in an Age of Too Much Information." *Columbia Journalism Review* (November/December 2008): 30–42.

Osnos, Peter. "What's a Fair Share in the Age of Google? How to Think about News in the Link Economy." *Columbia Journalism Review* (July/August 2009): 25–28: http://www.cjr.org/feature/whats_a_fair_share_in_the_age.php?page=all (accessed January 28, 2010).

Palser, Barb. "News à la Carte: An Increasingly Popular Online Tool Lets Consumers Control Their Media Diet, Receiving Headlines and Summaries in a Single Location." *American Journalism Review* 27, no. 1 (February/March 2005): 58.

Park, Robert E. "Urbanization as Measured by Newspaper Circulation." *American Journal of Sociology* 25 (1929): 60–79.

Peck, Abe, and Edward C. Malthouse, eds. *Medill on Media Engagement*. Cresskill, NJ: Hampton Press, forthcoming.

Peer, Limor. *User Engagement Study*. Evanston, IL: Media Management Center, June 2005: http://www.mediamanagementcenter.org/research/onlineoverview.pdf (accessed November 13, 2008).

Peer, Limor, Ed Malthouse, Mary Nesbitt, and Bobby Calder. *Local TV News Experience: How to Win Viewers by Focusing on Engagement*. Evanston, IL: Media Management Center, July 2007: http://mediamanagementcenter.org/research/localTV.pdf (accessed November 2, 2009).

Pérez-Peña, Richard. "Why Big Newspapers Applaud Some Declines in Circulation." *New York Times*, October 1, 2007: http://www.nytimes.com/2007/10/01/business/media/01paper.html (accessed November 29, 2009).

———. "Seattle Paper Is Resurgent as a Solo Act." *New York Times*, August 10, 2009: http://www.nytimes.com/2009/08/10/business/media/10seattle.html (accessed August 27, 2009).

———. "About Half in U.S. Would Pay for Online News, Study Finds." *New York Times*, November 16, 2009: http://www.nytimes.com/2009/11/16/business/media/16paywall.html (accessed November 16, 2009).

———. "Times to Stop Charging for Parts of Its Web Site." *New York Times*, September 18, 2007: http://www.nytimes.com/2007/09/18/business/media/18times.html (accessed April 6, 2010).

Pérez-Peña, Richard, and Tim Arango. "They Pay for Cable, Music and Extra Bags. How about News?" *New York Times*, April 8, 2009: http://www.nytimes.com/2009/04/08/business/media/08pay.html (accessed August 27, 2009).

Perkins, Douglas D., Paul Florin, Richard C. Roth, Abraham Wandersman, and David M. Chavis. "Participation and the Social and Physical Environment of Residential Blocks: Crime and Community Context." *American Journal of Community Psychology* 18, no. 1 (1990): 83–115.

Pew Internet and American Life Project. "Online News: For Many Home Broadband Users, the Internet Is a Primary News Source." March 22, 2006: http://www.pewinternet.org/PPF/r/178/report_display.asp (accessed March 23, 2006).

Pew Project for Excellence in Journalism. *The State of News Media 2006: An Annual Report on American Journalism*. Washington, D.C.: PEJ, 2006: http://www.stateofthenewsmedia.org/2006/narrative_online_intro.asp?media=4 (accessed October 9, 2006).

———. *The State of the News Media 2008: An Annual Report on American Journalism*. Washington, D.C.: PEJ, 2008: http://www.stateofthemedia.org/2008/ (accessed November 19, 2009).

———. *The State of the News Media 2009: An Annual Report on American Journalism*. Washington, D.C.: PEJ, 2009: http://www.stateofthemedia.org/2009/index.htm (accessed November 19, 2009).

Pew Research Center for People and the Press. *Social Networking and Online Videos Take Off: Internet's Broader Role in Campaign 2008*. Washington, D.C.: Pew

Research Center, January 11, 2008: http://people-press.org/reports/pdf/384.
pdf (accessed January 25, 2010).

———. *Who Moves? Who Stays Put? Where's Home?* Washington, D.C.: Pew
Research Center, 2008: http://pewsocialtrends.org/assets/pdf/Movers-and-
Stayers.pdf (accessed April 27, 2009).

———. *Majorities Say Right Amount on Leadership and Policies: Public Sees Too
Much Personal Coverage of Obama.* Washington, D.C.: Pew Research Cen-
ter, April 29, 2009: http://people-press.org/reports/pdf/512.pdf (accessed
October 7, 2009).

Picard, Robert G. "Commercialism and Newspaper Quality." *Newspaper Research
Journal* 25, no. 1 (2004): 54–65.

———. "Money, Media, and the Public Interest." In *The Press,* edited by Geneva
Overholser and Kathleen Hall Jamieson, 337–350. Oxford: Oxford University Press, 2005.

Pinch Media. "Paid Applications on the App Store (From 360iDev)." *Pinch
Media.com,* n.d.: http://www.pinchmedia.com/blog/paid-applications-on-
the-app-store-from-360idev/ (accessed December 16, 2009).

Price, Vincent. "Social Identification and Public Opinion: Effects of Communicating Group Conflict." *Public Opinion Quarterly* 53 (1989): 197–224.

Purdum, Tom S. "It Came from Wasilla." *Vanity Fair,* August 2009, 92–97, 139–144.

RealClearPolitics.com. "*RealClearPolitics*.com Launches New Web Site, Announces
Financing." News release, March 14, 2006: http://goliath.ecnext.com/coms2/
gi_0199-5320058/RealClearPolitics-com-Launches-New-Web.html (accessed January 27, 2010).

Roberts, Johnnie L. "Ebony: Up for Sale?" *Newsweek,* September 25, 2009: http://
www.newsweek.com/id/216176 (accessed December 3, 2009).

Rosen, Jay. *What Are Journalists For?* New Haven, CT: Yale University Press,
1999.

Rosenberg, Scott. "The Post's Public Enemy Gaffe: Why Circle-the-Wagons Is a
Joke." *Idea Lab,* December 17, 2009: http://www.pbs.org/idealab/2009/12/
the-posts-public-enemy-gaffe-why-circle-the-wagons-is-a-joke350.html
(accessed January 18, 2010).

Rubin, Rebecca B., Alan M. Rubin, Elizabeth M. Perse, Cameron B. Armstrong,
Michael P. McHugh, and Noreen Faix. "Media Use and Meaning of Music
Video." *Journalism Quarterly* 63 (1986): 353–359.

Ruggiero, Thomas E., and Kenneth Yang. "Latino Ethnic Identity, Linguistic Ac-
culturation, and Spanish Language Media Preference." Paper presented
at the annual meeting of the International Communication Association
Conference, New York, May 2005.

Sanoff, Alvin P. "TV News Growing Too Powerful?" *U.S. News & World Report,*
June 9, 1980, 59.

Sarason, Seymour B. *The Psychological Sense of Community: Prospects for Community Psychology.* San Francisco: Jossey-Bass, 1974.

Schaefer, Ian. "DigitalNext: Facebook Connect." *Advertising Age* 80, no. 4 (February 2, 2009): 21.

Schmidt, Eric. "How Google Can Help Save Newspapers." *Wall Street Journal*, December 1, 2009: http://online.wsj.com/article/SB100014240527487041 07104574569570797550520.html (accessed January 27, 2010).

Shapira, Ian. "The Death of Journalism (*Gawker* Edition)." *Washington Post*, August 2, 2009: http://www.washingtonpost.com/wp-dyn/content/article/2009/07/31/AR2009073102476.html (accessed January 28, 2010).

Sherman, Gabriel. "Post Apocalypse: Inside the Messy Collapse of a Great Newspaper." *New Republic*, January 19, 2010: http://www.tnr.com/article/politics/post-apocalypse (accessed January 25, 2010).

Siebert, Fred S., Theodore Peterson, and Wilbur Schramm. *Four Theories of the Press: The Authoritarian, Libertarian, Social Responsibility and Soviet Communist Concepts of What the Press Should Be and Do*. Urbana: University of Illinois Press, 1963.

Sifry, Micah L. "A See-through Society." *Columbia Journalism Review* (January/February 2009): 43–47.

Smith, Aaron, Kay Lehman Schlozman, Sidney Verba, and Henry Brady. *The Internet and Civic Engagement*. Washington, D.C.: Pew Internet and American Life Project, September 2009: http://pewinternet.org/Reports/2009/15—The-Internet-and-Civic-Engagement/1—Summary-of-Findings.aspx?r=1 (accessed December 6, 2009).

Stamm, Keith. *Community Ties and Newspaper Use: Toward a Dynamic Theory*. Norwood, NJ: Ablex, 1985.

Stepp, Carl Sessions. "Journalism without Profit Margins." *American Journalism Review* 26, no. 5 (2004): 38.

Stone, Gerald C., Donna B. Stone, and Edgar P. Trotter. "Newspaper Quality's Relation to Circulation." *Newspaper Research Journal* 2 (1981): 16–24.

Tajfel, Henri. "Social Identity and Intergroup Behavior." *Social Science Information* 13, no. 2 (April 1974): 65–93.

Tewksbury, David, and Scott L. Althaus. "An Examination of Motivations for Using the World Wide Web." *Communication Research Reports* 17, no. 2 (Spring 2000): 127–138.

Thurlow, George L., and Katherine J. Milo. "Newspaper Readership: Can the Bleeding Be Stopped, or Do We Have the Wrong Patient?" *Newspaper Research Journal* 14, no. 3 (1993): 34–44.

Time. "Radio: Why Do They Like It?" *Time*, June 29, 1942: http://www.time.com/time/magazine/article/0,9171,795946,00.html (accessed November 3, 2009).

Urista, Mark A., Dong Qingwne, and Kenneth D. Day. "Explaining Why Young Adults Use MySpace and Facebook through Uses and Gratifications Theory." *Human Communication* 12, no. 2 (Summer 2009): 215–229.

USC Annenberg News. "Annual Internet Survey by Center for the Digital Future Finds Large Increases in Use of Online Newspapers." News release, April 29, 2009: http://annenberg.usc.edu/AboutUs/News/090429CDF.aspx (accessed November 29, 2009).

Vincent, Richard C., and Michael D. Basil. "College Students' News Gratifications, Media Use, and Current Events Knowledge." *Journal of Broadcasting and Electronic Media* 41, no. 3 (1997): 380–392.

Walsh, Mark. "Nielsen: Smartphones to Be Majority of Cell Phones by 2011." *MediaPost*, November 12, 2009: http://www.mediapost.com/publications/?fa=Articles.showArticle&art_aid=117275 (accessed January 24, 2010).

Washington Post. "The *Washington Post* Launches Facebook Connect." News release, June 15, 2009: http://www.washingtonpost.com/wp-adv/media_kit/wp/press_releases/the_washington_post_launches_facebook_connect.html (accessed October 19, 2009).

———. "Correction." December 3, 2009: http://www.washingtonpost.com/wp-dyn/content/article/2009/12/02/AR2009120201455.html (accessed December 17, 2009).

Watson, Warren. "Smile? Celebrity News Reaches Young Readers, but Some Editors Wonder If the Cost Is Too High." *The American Editor* (August/September/October 2005): 4–9.

Wetpaint and Altimeter. *The World's Most Valuable Brands: Who's Most Engaged?* July 2009: http://www.engagementdb.com/downloads/ENGAGEMENTdb_Report_2009.pdf (accessed January 23, 2010).

Wilkinson, Earl J. "Content's Monetary Value Determined by Content, Audience, Source Segmentations." *The Earl Blog: Connecting the Dots for the Global Newsmedia Industry*, August 26, 2009: http://www.inma.org/modules/blog/index.cfm?action=blog_detail&bid=73 (accessed August 27, 2009).

———. "Role of Audiences in Corporate Strategy Will Determine Publisher Success in Decade Ahead." *The Earl Blog: Connecting the Dots for the Global Newsmedia Industry,* December 22, 2009: http://www.inma.org/modules/blog/index.cfm?action=blog_detail&bid=\90 (accessed January 24, 2010).

Wolcott, James. "What's a Culture Snob to Do?" *Vanity Fair*, August 2009, 68–71.

Wolf, Katherine M., and Marjorie Fiske. "The Children Talk about Comics." In *Communication Research*, edited by Paul F. Lazarsfeld and Frank N. Stanton, 3–50. New York: Harper & Brothers, 1949.

Wolff, Michael. "Post Modern," *Vanity Fair*, October 2009: http://www.vanityfair.com/business/features/2009/10/wolff200910 (accessed October 31, 2009).

Woodruff, Judy. "Are Journalists Obsolete?" *PoynterOnline*, January 12, 2007: http://www.poynter.org/content/content_view.asp?id=130871 (accessed April 15, 2010).

Yuan, Jada. "Mort Zuckerman's Plan to Save Newspapers." *New York*, May 6, 2009: http://nymag.com/daily/intel/2009/05/mort_zuckerman.html (accessed August 27, 2009).

Zeeck, David A. "ASNE President's Speech." Annual convention of the American Society of Newspaper Editors, Washington, D.C., March 2007.

Index

About the Author

RACHEL DAVIS MERSEY is an assistant professor of the Medill School of Journalism at Northwestern University, where she is also a fellow in the Institute for Policy Research. She teaches undergraduate and graduate courses exploring the changing nature of people's relationships with media and the applicability of audience research to the practice of journalism. Her research focuses on the influence of digital media on newspapers' community-building function, identity salience and media use, and the information needs of particular audiences. Before earning her PhD at the University of North Carolina-Chapel Hill, she worked as a reporter at the *Arizona Republic* in Phoenix.